DATE DUE

Nigeria

Nigeria

BY ETTAGALE BLAUER
AND JASON LAURÉ

Enchantment of the World
Second Series

Children's Press®

A Division of Scholastic Inc.

NEW YORK   TORONTO   LONDON   AUCKLAND   SYDNEY
MEXICO CITY   NEW DELHI   HONG KONG
DANBURY, CONNECTICUT

Frontispiece: A Hausa girl has tribal tattoos and wears traditional clothing and headdress of her tribe.

Consultant: Dr. Jon Kraus, Department of Political Science, SUNY/Fredonia, New York

Please note: All statistics are as up-to-date as possible at the time of publication.

Visit Children's Press on the Internet: http://publishing.grolier.com

Book Production by Herman Adler Design

Library of Congress Cataloging-in-Publication Data

Blauer, Ettagale and Lauré, Jason
    Nigeria / by Ettagale Blauer and Jason Lauré.
      p. cm. — (Enchantment of the world. Second series)
    Includes bibliographical references and index.
    ISBN 0-516-22281-3
    1. Nigeria—Juvenile literature. [1. Nigeria.] I. Lauré, Jason. II. Title. III. Series.
    DT515.22 .B54 2001
    966.9—dc21   00-065597

Acknowledgments

We would like to thank the many people who helped us to understand the people and customs of Nigeria. It is not always the case that you get to know, by name, someone who gives you a glimpse into a culture. We would like to thank especially Olanike Olakunri, Laolu Akande, and David Dorward for their help in our research.

Cover photo:
Nigerian man in
traditional clothing

Contents

Returning from market

A Yoruba bronze

Struggling with Democracy

IN FEBRUARY 1999, PEOPLE THROUGHOUT NIGERIA WENT to voting booths and elected a new president—Olusegun Obasanjo. Three months later, he was sworn into office as the leader of the country with the largest population in Africa. Many leaders of other nations attended the ceremony to show their support for the democratic process taking place in Nigeria.

Opposite: **Two women count votes in a recent election.**

President Olusegun Obasanjo (left) shakes hands with General Abubakar, the outgoing military ruler.

In its first forty years as a nation, Nigeria has known only ten years of democracy. Each time a national government was elected under the laws of the Constitution, military officers would seize control of the government within four or five years. Then the country would exist under a military dictatorship. These were not peaceful periods for Nigeria. Factions within the military fought with each other for control of the nation.

A market scene shows the variety of food and clothing of Nigeria.

Why does Nigeria have so much trouble keeping its civilian leadership? Part of the reason is the country's ethnic diversity. Nigeria has more cultures, or peoples, within its borders than any other nation in Africa. An elected president has a difficult task—to bring together a country that has more than 250 ethnic groups who speak as many as 400 languages. Nigeria's people are also divided by their religious beliefs. Many people are Christians, while many others are Muslims.

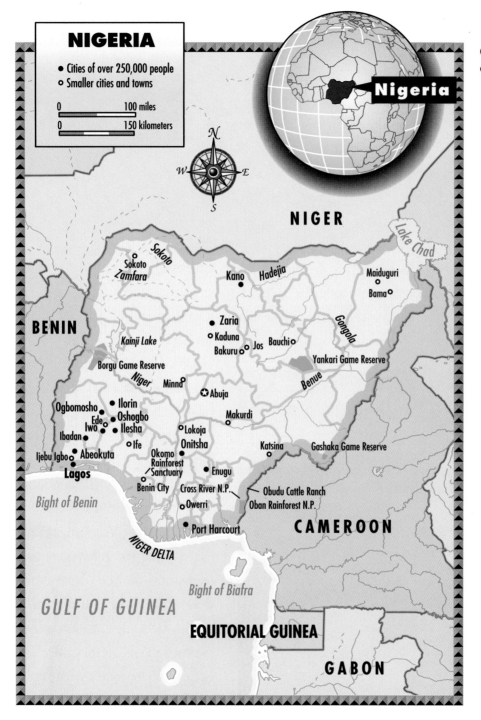

Geopolitical map of Nigeria

Nigeria inherited these problems from its earliest days. Great Britain colonized Nigeria and drew the borders of the country in 1914. The borders enclosed a great many people who had no interest in being part of the same country. When Nigeria gained its independence, Nigerians soon found out that being a nation takes more than choosing a flag, an anthem, and a president. Since its independence on October 1, 1960, Nigeria has bumped along a rocky road, searching for a peaceful way to govern its people.

Nigeria has enormous economic wealth, but this money does not improve the lives of most of the people. The country receives a huge income from oil, found in the Niger Delta. Yet the Nigerian people remain extremely poor.

An oil refinery

Will Nigerians give President Obasanjo the time he needs to solve the problems that divide the nation? The United States is betting that Nigeria will succeed. The United States considers Nigeria to be very important for two major reasons. First, it wants to see democracy flourish in Africa, and Nigeria could become an excellent example of democracy in action. If democracy triumphs in Nigeria, then other African nations will most likely turn to democracy as well. Another reason is that the United States buys 8 percent of its oil from Nigeria. The United States doesn't want to lose this source of oil. Just before the end of his term in office, President Bill Clinton paid a visit to Nigeria to show U.S. support for President Obasanjo. At the same time, the United States agreed to help train the Nigerian army in its peacekeeping mission in Africa. Nigeria needs peace in the region in order to have peace and security at home.

U.S. president Bill Clinton walks through a Nigerian village during his visit to Africa in 2000.

Soldier on a peacekeeping mission

The Land and Its People

To find Nigeria on a map of Africa, look at the big bulge that forms West Africa. Then follow the Atlantic Ocean coastline until you reach the Gulf of Guinea. There you will find Nigeria, which sits right on the gulf. Nigeria has a land area of 365,695 square miles (923,768 square kilometers). It is more than twice the size of the state of California.

Several countries border Nigeria. Niger is Nigeria's northern neighbor. Benin lies to the west, while Cameroon is located on the east. Lake Chad forms the country's northeast corner. The neighboring country of Chad is located on the other side of this lake

From the Atlantic Ocean, the land rises gently in a series of plateaus that make up a sort of giant staircase. The land, which is at sea level along the coast, increases from south to north to about 2,000 feet (100 meters), 3,000 feet (900 m), and 4,000 feet (1,200 m). The highest areas are found on the Jos Plateau, in the center of the country, and along the Cameroon border. The highest point in Nigeria is Dimlang Peak, measuring 6,699 feet (2,042 m) in the Cameroon Highlands.

Opposite: **The Niger River**

Jos Plateau

Nigeria's Geographical Features

Area: 356,695 square miles (923,768 sq km)

Highest Elevation: Dimlang Peak at 6,699 feet (2,042 m) in the Cameroon Highlands

Lowest Elevation: Sea level along the Gulf of Guinea.

Longest River: Niger River, 650 miles (1,046 km)

Largest Delta: Niger Delta, 14,000 square miles (36,250 sq km)

Greatest Annual Precipitation: 160 inches (406 cm) along the southeast coast

Lowest Annual Precipitation: 20 inches (50 cm) in the north

Highest Average Temperature: 100 degrees Fahrenheit (38 degrees Celsius) in Maiduguri

Lowest Average Temperature: 68°F (20°C) in Port Harcourt

Longest Shared Border: With Cameroon, 1,050 miles (1,690 km)

Greatest Distance North to South: 650 miles (1,046 km)

Greatest Distance East to West: 800 miles (1,287 km)

Coastline: 478 miles (769 km)

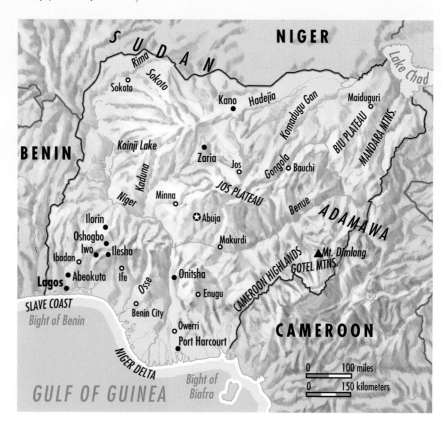

Most of southern Nigeria is covered by mountainless land called a coastal plain. The flat surface begins at the shore and continues inland. This plain is divided by a huge swampy region called the Niger Delta.

Beyond the coastal plain, the land extends northward along two river basins, the Niger River to the west and the Benue River to the east. The country's name comes from the Niger River.

As you move northward, the amount of rainfall decreases so that there are fewer areas of heavy vegetation or concentrations of trees. The northern half of the country is marked by wide plateaus and small granite mountains. The extreme northern area of the country touches the edge of the Sahara Desert, a region known as the *Sahel*, which means "fringe" in Arabic.

Fulani people depend on their livestock to survive in the harsh climate of the north.

A boy paddles his boat on the brown waters of the Niger River.

Niger River

The Niger River is often called the "Strong Brown God" because it is a powerful and important river and because it is colored brown with silt. The Niger begins its life in the country of Guinea and runs eastward through the countries of Mali and Niger before it enters Nigeria. It continues flowing to the southeast until it meets the Benue River at Lokoja, a town in central Nigeria. The waters of the Benue rush into the Niger and double the volume of the river. It continues on as the Niger, now spreading across the landscape to a width of about 2 miles (3 km). This mighty river travels directly to the south until it empties into the Gulf of Guinea.

When the Niger River is about 60 miles (100 km) from the coast, it forms the Niger Delta, sprawling out into one of the world's largest wetlands, covering an area about 200 miles (320 km) along the coast. The delta is a swampy region where mangrove trees rise up from the water. Today, it is best known as the source of Nigeria's oil reserves as well as natural gas deposits. It is the place where some of the worst pollution and human rights abuses occur in Nigeria.

Where's the River?

The Niger and the Benue, like many rivers in Africa, vary in size during the year. As water flows into the Niger from upstream, the river increases in volume and in depth. During the dry season, the level of the water drops. At this time, river traffic comes to a halt in some sections of the river because there is not enough water to carry the boats along. During the wet season, more water flows into the Niger from upstream. The river increases in volume and depth, and its currents can become very fast. Traveling by boat during the wet season can be dangerous.

Passengers travel in canoes and ferries on the Niger River.

The lives of the people change during the dry season and the wet season. During the dry season, especially, water is precious to Nigerians. People depend on boats to bring them supplies. Only a short stretch of the river is deep enough for large boats. For most of its great length, only small boats can navigate the river at any time, even during the rainy season. Rivers and lakes are the lifeblood of the people. They provide water for drinking, cooking, washing, and bathing.

Sunset on Lake Chad

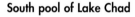

South pool of Lake Chad

Lake Chad

Rivers that come and go aren't the only water sources in Nigeria. Lake Chad, in the northeast corner, has been doing a real disappearing act for more than forty years. This lake once covered 10,000 square miles (25,000 square kilometers). Now, it has shrunk to about one-tenth that size and there are fears that it will dry up entirely. If that happens, it will cause tremendous harm for the 9 million people who depend on the lake for fishing and for watering their herds of livestock. Many of these people live in Nigeria.

The lake is drying up because the Sahel, the southern edge of the Sahara, is creeping south. A little at a time, the desert is slowly growing and swallowing up the lake.

Weather

The weather in Nigeria changes as you move northward from the coastline along the Gulf of Guinea. As you travel farther north, the climate becomes drier. In Nigeria, just as in most parts of Africa, the weather is measured by rainfall, not by whether it's hot or cold. There are rainy seasons and dry seasons, and they form the major weather systems. Along the coast and in the southeast, the rainy season usually begins in February or March. The rain comes with high winds as well.

The rainy season moves north as the year progresses. By April or May, rain has reached the valleys of the Niger and Benue Rivers. In the very north of the country, the rains may not start until June or July. Because the period of rainfall is short, the growing season is also very short. In this region, there is a time called the "hunger season," when food grown previously has been used and the next crop is not ready to be harvested. Most people are too poor to buy food from other regions.

In September through November, when the winds begin to blow from the northeast, Nigeria starts to enjoy lower humidity. However, in December these same winds bring the dust of the Sahara, which lies just to the north. The local name for this wind is the *harmattan*. It is a powerful wind that can hurl a fine coating of sand over an entire region. The harmattan rules people's lives—it directs the kinds of houses they build, whether they can grow crops, and whether they have drinking water.

Rain usually falls most heavily in the south and then less and less to the north. It rains more than 157 inches (400 cm)

Lagos, the largest city, on a rainy day

along parts of the coast and as little as 20 inches (50 cm) in the north. The length of the rainy season also decreases as you move north. In Kano, the rainy season lasts for 120–130 days.

Whether or not it is raining, the temperature is likely to be high. The difference between daytime and nighttime temperatures is often dramatic, especially in the north. The desert like conditions in the north can mean blisteringly hot days with a sharp drop of 40°F (4°C) at night. Night is sometimes called the "winter of the desert." The land does not hold the daytime heat.

How Many People?

There is no question that Nigeria has the largest population of any country in Africa, but the exact number of people has always been debated. For most of Nigeria's existence as an independent nation, there has not been a census that was widely accepted. The problem lies in the division between the north and the south. The north, which is generally Muslim, has a higher population and is growing at a faster rate than the south, where most people follow Christianity or traditional religion.

Many people fear that if Nigerian officials took an accurate census, the Muslim north would turn out to have many more people than expected. Then that section of the country would

have more representation and power in the government. The importance of the census in determining representation is similar to that of the United States. Every ten years, the number of representatives from the states is adjusted to show the changes in population distribution. As a result, Nigeria's population figures sometimes seem to be going down instead of up. The population figures also seem to indicate that one part of the country may have no population growth for ten years at a time while another grows by leaps and bounds.

Three different estimates were given for the 1999–2000 period: 113,828,587 people, 139,420,000 people, and 128,790,000 people. In the year 2000, the generally accepted figure was 118,800,000. The normal method of estimating how many people will be living in Nigeria in the next twenty-five years has become almost useless since AIDS began to affect the people of Africa. While Nigeria does not have the highest rate of AIDS deaths, it is likely to lose many of its citizens to this disease.

Looking at Nigerian Cities

Ibadan (pictured), Nigeria's second-largest city, is located about 100 miles (160 km) inland from Lagos. Its name means "field between the plain and the savanna." Ibadan was founded at the end of the 1700s by the Yoruba people. Under British colonial rule, Ibadan became an important trading center. Today, the New Dugbe Market is one of Nigeria's largest markets. The Oje Market is one of the largest cloth markets in Africa, and the Bode Market specializes in beads. The main industries in Ibadan produce furniture and plastics. The city also has the University of Ibadan, one of West Africa's best schools. Scientists at the Institute of Tropical Agriculture study the cassava, yam, and other foods that are basic to the West African diet. Ibadan has warm weather year-round. January temperatures average 80°F (27°C); July temperatures, 75°F (24°C). About 45 inches (114 cm) of rain falls on Ibadan each year.

Kano, Nigeria's third-largest city, is located in north-central Nigeria. It was founded over 1,000 years ago by the Hausa people. Today, the population is mainly Hausa with many Fulani. The city is a major trading center for northern Nigeria, shipping food products, leather and hides, peanuts, and textiles. The Kurmi Market attracts many tourists with its gold,

bronze, and silver work and many types of fabrics. Also of interest is the Old City with traditional Hausa architecture, the Central Mosque, and the Emir's Palace. Kano enjoys an average January temperature of 70°F (21°C) and an average July temperature of 79°F (26°C). The city's annual rainfall averages 35 inches (89 cm).

Ogbomosho, Nigeria's fourth-largest city, is northeast of Ibadan. It was founded in the mid-1600s and resisted Fulani invasions in the 1800s. Today, Ogbomosho is a trade center and highway junction that ships foodstuffs, livestock, and tobacco.

Why does a country need to know how many people are living in each area? Knowing how the population is distributed helps the government decide how to spend money, where to build roads, and where it will need more schools and hospitals. Without accurate information, planning is based on guesswork.

It is generally agreed that Nigeria is home to about 15 percent of all the people in Africa. It also has the most diverse mix of people of any nation on the continent. When Great Britain colonized Nigeria, it drew borders for the nation that brought together anywhere from 200 to 400 ethnic groups and tribes. Because these groups speak so many different languages, language is the main method of identification. The British also forced Nigerians to learn English, introducing it as the language used in government, commerce, and education. Today, businesspeople usually speak English as well as their own language. Most Nigerians in the rural areas speak their own language, not English.

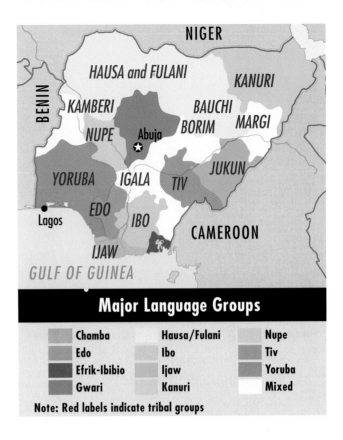

Major Language Groups

Chamba	Hausa/Fulani	Nupe
Edo	Ibo	Tiv
Efrik-Ibibio	Ijaw	Yoruba
Gwari	Kanuri	Mixed

Note: Red labels indicate tribal groups

The three main ethnic groups—making up about 70 to 75 percent of the total population—live in different geographical areas although there has been some migration among them. The Hausa are found in the northern half of the country while the Yoruba live in the southwest and the Igbo in the southeast. The Fulani, a nomadic group, has mixed with the Hausa to a large extent, and can be found widely throughout the northern region. People often refer to them as the Hausa-Fulani.

Hausa father and his son stand in a field.

Disappearing
Nature

When we think of Africa, our first thoughts are often of its magnificent animals and splendid scenery. In Nigeria, only a few fragments remain of the region's original natural glory, and those bits are very threatened. Although the country does have several national parks and game reserves, they have almost no facilities and scarcely any wildlife. Tourists find the going very tough in Nigeria.

Traditional tourism, for people who stay in first-class hotels and travel on scheduled tours, is really not the way to go in Nigeria. Most of the travel is done by casual travelers, called backpackers. They are better suited to Nigeria's challenging travel conditions. Groups traveling by Land Rover and truck across Africa are among the few people to enter Nigeria overland from the Sahara. Carrying all their own water, gasoline and food, they are able to see how people live.

Most of Nigeria's wildlife disappeared a long time ago. Many forests and wetlands where wildlife once lived have been taken for farming by Nigeria's rapidly growing population. The number of animals declined as their habitats shrunk. Nearly all of the remaining wildlife can be found in Yankari National Park.

Opposite: **Livestock graze in a savanna near the Jos Plateau.**

Yankari National Park is known for its mammals and birds.

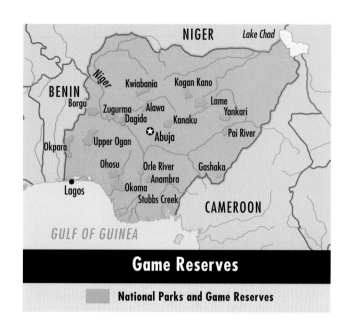

Game Reserves

National Parks and Game Reserves

While a number of areas are designated as national parks, Yankari National Park is the one that has the most facilities. Like the other park areas, it is known for its birds. However, this park also features large mammals—elephants, waterbuck, and bushbuck. Monkeys, baboons, and crocodiles are also found in Yankari. In most parks of Nigeria, the large mammals have been wiped out, including cheetahs, giraffes, black rhinos, and giant eland. Yankari also has natural springs called Wikki Warm Springs.

Rain forest in the southeast

Established in 1845, Okumu Nature Sanctuary is not far from Benin City. This park has one of the few remaining areas of rain forest, as well as white-throated monkeys and some elephants. The main attraction here is the bird life.

Cross River National Park, in the southeast part of the country, shares a border with a national park in neighboring Cameroon. It also has rain forest and many kinds of birds. It is even said to have rare, endangered gorillas. However, the Ikrigon Forest Reserve, which is part of Cross River National Park, is threatened by logging. The logging was approved by the state government. The World Wide Fund for Nature and the Nigerian Conservation Foundation manage the park.

Gashaka Gumpti

Founded in 1991, Gashaka Gumpti National Park is the largest national park in Nigeria. Located in the southeastern part of the country, near the border with Cameroon, this park has a wide variety of terrain from grasslands to mountain forest. Because some of the major tributaries of the Benue River are found here, these forested mountains are vital. If these water sources are lost due to logging, millions of people in Nigeria will lose their source of water. The Oban Rainforest Reserve lies within the park where visitors can hike.

Visitors who make their way to the park can search for elephants, hippos, waterbuck, and buffalo, but there is no guarantee that they will be seen. The animals have so much room to move around in that it's easy for them to hide. When visitors get to the park, they must hire a "bush taxi," which is a rough vehicle that can manage the dirt roads. Visitors also have to carry all their food and water with them because they won't be able to buy anything once they leave the main lodge of the park.

Birds Still Abound

Nine hundred species of birds have been identified within the borders of Nigeria. This area is a potentially great destination for bird-watchers. However, it will take considerable effort to repair roads, build lodges, and train park rangers and other staff to make this possible.

A little Nubian nightjar rests on the ground.

An African grey parrot perches on a tree branch.

The lack of facilities has not stopped smugglers, who continue to go after birds, especially the African grey parrot. This intelligent bird sports a brilliant scarlet tail and is a favorite in pet shops. Poachers—people who capture or kill animals and birds illegally—don't care if they capture so many animals that the entire species is wiped out. They are concerned about making money, and there is a lot of money to be made in smuggling wildlife out of Nigeria. A grey parrot, for example, sells for about U.S.$500 in Europe and in the United States.

Mangrove Forests

Along Nigeria's southern coast, great forests of mangroves were once an important part of the environment. Mangrove trees live in watery, muddy places called *wetlands*. The trees may

Mangrove forest

be small, the size of bushes, or they may reach 100–130 feet (30–40 m) in height. People often use wood from mangrove trees to build their houses and as fuel for their cooking fires. They use the leaves to thatch the roofs of their houses.

Mangrove trees serve several purposes in nature. They create a place where fish can find food, they provide vital elements to clean the air, and they help to break up ocean waves before they reach land. Animals live in the mangrove forests and along the shores. When any part of this system is tipped out of balance, the whole environment suffers.

Nigeria's mangrove forest is considered the third largest in the world. These forests are found all along the shore, but most of them are in the Niger Delta. Although almost all dryland forests in Nigeria have been cut down, mangrove forests still stand. Where mangrove forests have been destroyed, it is mainly due to people moving into the area or pollution from oil pumping.

The Problem with Oil

The Niger River was an important source of fish until the discovery of oil. Oil pollution has killed off most of the fish and has made life very difficult for the people who once depended on fish for food. Oil spills, from the pipelines that carry the oil, or from damaged equipment at the oil pumping sites, seep into the soil and water, and pollute the air. For decades, the Ogoni people have been fighting the international oil companies that drill for oil.

**Mangrove swamps
outside Lagos**

To have a healthy mangrove forest, the swampy region must be washed regularly by the ebb and flow of water. This movement of water scrubs the area, mixes up the silt, and creates food for the roots of the trees.

Dams have been built on the Niger and Benue Rivers to create electricity. These dams have changed the ebb and flow of water, which takes place during the rainy seasons. If the delta is not washed by the seasonal floods, the ecosystem can be destroyed. Too much silt also interferes with transportation since the only way to travel in the region is by boat. Big boats that carry hundreds of people, as well as smaller boats used for fishing, are common sights in the region.

Losing the Forests

Although Nigeria is rich in oil—producing about 2 million barrels a day—most people rely on wood for their daily cooking needs. Less than 10 percent of Nigeria is still covered with forest. The southern rain forest that contains valuable timber, however, covers only 2 percent of the land and is disappearing quickly.

In spite of this, former governments granted foreigners the right to cut down trees in the tropical rain forest. The local people also cut down trees, clearing forests to use as farmland and burning the wood to make cooking fires. As the population grows, more and more of the forests will be cut down. The World Wide Fund for Nature estimates that if conservation efforts aren't put into effect immediately, all of Nigeria's forests will be gone by the year 2010.

Logs stacked along a river-bank in the rain forest

A Long and
Noble History

36

M The Great Kingdoms

ORE THAN 2,000 YEARS AGO, LONG BEFORE THE invention of electricity and computers, automobiles and television, wonderful cultures flourished in Nigeria. In some cases, we know little more than the names of these early peoples.

Nigeria's earliest residents lived in well-established communities, led by people who were called *obas* or *onis*. One of these groups is called the Nok people. From around 500 B.C. to A.D. 200, they lived near Jos, north of where the Benue and Niger Rivers meet. Their beautiful sculptures of terra-cotta, a form of clay that has been hardened by firing it in an oven, tell us how these people lived. No other people in the region came close to the Nok's level of skill and development for another thousand years.

About A.D. 1000, the Yoruba people lived in villages that grew into city-states. They occupied a vast region to the west of the Niger River, extending more than 200 miles (322 km) from east to west. They were also skilled in working with bronze. They were part of extensive trade routes that were developing in the region. Their trading center was known as Ife.

The Benin kingdom, in southern Nigeria, developed more than 600 years ago. At least 100,000 people lived in Benin around the fifteenth century.

Opposite: **Realistic bronze head made by the Yoruba people**

A finely-crafted Yoruba bronze object

They left behind beautifully detailed heads that they cast in bronze. These bronzes are among the most treasured objects from ancient Africa, and they provide an idea of how people looked, the way the women braided their hair, and who their important leaders were.

Hausa Kingdom

Around the same time, in the north of Nigeria, the Hausa kingdom was thriving. Kano and Katsina, major cities of the kingdom, were flourishing centers of trade. These were not entirely peaceful times. The trade routes also brought aggressive peoples seeking to conquer the Hausa. They introduced the Hausa to the Muslim religion. Fulani nomads, who roamed an enormous region of West Africa, were known in northern Nigeria by the thirteenth century.

Kano

Later, invaders from the great Songhai Empire, which covered a vast region in West Africa, came into Nigeria and took parts of Hausaland. Then the Borno kingdom conquered the rest of the Hausa region. They were the most powerful force in the area that is present-day Nigeria for the next 200 years.

During this time, the Hausa people constantly fought for power among themselves. This constant strife, as well as military threats from other people in the region, ended the Songhai and Borno control of the Hausa.

Finally, a great drought—a period of little or no rain—in the mid-1700s caused a terrible famine, perhaps the worst that has ever occurred in Nigeria. This catastrophe ended the Borno's power altogether.

Enter the Europeans

Five hundred years ago, the Portuguese were a great sailing people. They had the ability to navigate the seas, explore other countries, and then return safely home to Portugal. With their sailing skills, they set in motion the ultimate conquest of Africa by the European powers. They also set the stage for the kind of slavery that saw millions of Africans put on ships to wind up in North and South America.

Plaque showing Portuguese traders

Statue of a Portuguese soldier holding a gun

Slave trading on the west coast of Africa

The Slave Trade

By 1471, the Portuguese had arrived on the coast of Nigeria, reaching the Niger Delta. They quickly established relations with the oba of Benin and began a very profitable trade. The Benin wanted the objects the Europeans made, especially tools and weapons. The Portuguese wanted ivory, peppers, and slaves. In those days there were no refrigerators to keep meat from spoiling, so peppers were crucial for preserving meat. Finding a source for peppers was the main reason for many sailing expeditions.

The more weapons the oba wanted from the Portuguese, the more slaves he delivered to them. The weapons allowed the Benin to maintain control in their region. Although the Benin decided to stop exporting people as slaves, they continued to use slaves among their own villages. Once the

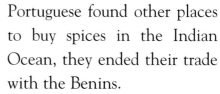

Portuguese found other places to buy spices in the Indian Ocean, they ended their trade with the Benins.

Slavery, however, didn't stop. The Portuguese simply went to other kingdoms along the coast where they could trade for a supply of captives. Soon, other European powers, including the Dutch, the French, and the British, also started to buy and sell slaves.

In time, the British became the most important slaving power in the region. During the eighteenth century, Nigeria supplied the most slaves, in part because it was easier for the slave traders to operate there.

No one knows how many Africans were forced into slavery. Estimates range from 10 million to 30 million people. A third of these people were shipped out of Nigeria. If the African chiefs had not been so willing to sacrifice other Africans, the slave trade would not have grown to such huge numbers.

After slavery was banned by the British, and later in the United States, it did not disappear from Nigerian society. Instead, slaves were used locally in the growing palm-oil business and in farming. Palm-oil products eventually replaced slavery as a source of wealth in the Niger Delta.

The various African peoples living in Nigeria continued to form alliances throughout the period. However, these alliances seemed to fall apart as quickly as they were formed. Local customs and beliefs were well known and respected, often guaranteed by treaties. Markets were the great gathering places where goods were traded and people came into contact with one another. Some people prospered because of the slave trade, especially the Ijaw. Living along the coast, they became middlemen in the slave trade, creating a source of wealth they never enjoyed before.

Confined to the Coast

In the early 1800s, missionaries came into West Africa. They planned to convert the Africans to the Christian religion and set up churches and schools. By 1850, many Yoruba leaders had signed peace treaties with the British.

Nigeria's coastal city of Lagos became a British colony in 1861. After that, the British peacefully took over all of Yorubaland except Ijebu. Although the Yoruba of Ijebu greatly outnumbered the British, they were no match for the British rifles and machine guns. The British fought hard against the Ijebu, because they wanted other Yoruba groups to believe that there was no way they could win.

Although the British had explored the coast, the interior of Nigeria was a great mystery to them. They knew of the great Niger River, but not of its final course. They did not understand the geography beyond the Niger Delta. Each time the British tried to establish trade farther inland, their attempts failed. Malaria and the hot, humid climate struck down at least one-third of the members of these expeditions.

The British continued to conduct business in the cities along the coast. The best-known business was the United Africa Company, which was started by George Goldie in 1879. The British also gave Goldie permission to form the Royal Niger Company. He had the right to trade in the whole Niger basin. The British didn't ask permission from the African people who had lived in the region for centuries, though. Goldie's company grew very powerful and became a political force in the region.

British Take Over

Little did the people of present-day Nigeria guess that, far away in Europe, several nations were making deals that greatly concerned them. In 1885, Germany, France, and England met at the Conference of Berlin, in Germany, to discuss how they should divide Africa. It was the beginning of the scramble for European control of the continent.

A British steamship salutes the canoe of an African chief.

After the conference, cultures that had lived in certain regions for centuries suddenly found themselves governed by European powers. Thanks to Goldie's businesses, England claimed most of Nigeria. France claimed most of Nigeria's neighboring regions to the north, east, and west.

There was one positive side to this takeover. Much of the warfare that had occurred between African states and communities came to an end. The Europeans also introduced medical knowledge and sanitation that helped to reduce the diseases that had been part of everyday life.

Claiming the North

By 1897, most of southern Nigeria had come under British control. In other parts of Nigeria, however, traders and missionaries had not become so much a part of the British society. The north, in particular, was ruled by *emirs*, leaders of the Islamic regions known as *emirates*. They had resisted the missionaries and remained true to their own religion. The traders they dealt with were not connected to the Europeans.

The church missionary station at Badagry, in the south

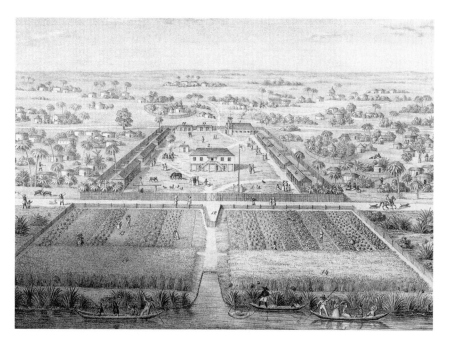

This painting shows the massacre of a British mission in Benin in 1897.

There was a reason for the British rushing to conquer the northern area quickly. They wanted to keep out France and Germany, two other European countries that were quickly claiming other parts of Africa. Between 1897 and 1903, the British conquered one area after another. They fought with guns, rifles, and cannons. The local people fought with spears, arrows, and swords, which were no match for the modern weapons. Unlike in the south, the leaders of the north did not give in after they saw one ruler defeated. Each one fought to save his own people and his own land. They were not united in their fighting. It was a very unequal struggle, and the British always won.

The great civilizations of the Hausa states, including Sokoto and Kano, either lost these military battles, or gave up

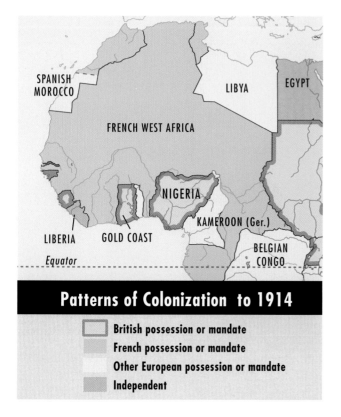

SPANISH MOROCCO

LIBYA

EGYPT

FRENCH WEST AFRICA

NIGERIA

KAMEROON (Ger.)

LIBERIA   GOLD COAST

BELGIAN CONGO

Equator

Patterns of Colonization to 1914

☐ British possession or mandate

French possession or mandate

Other European possession or mandate

Independent

Frederick Lugard

their independence in the face of overwhelming odds. However, they never gave up the idea of someday being independent again.

Now, the Yoruba, the Hausa, the Igbo and all the other ethnic groups had to learn to exist as part of the British Protectorate of Nigeria, which was created in 1914. They had to learn how to live as members of a British colony.

Indirect Rule

Although the British wanted to maintain control of Nigeria, they were not interested in sending in thousands of men to run the colony. The weather was too severe. Diseases, such as malaria, were devastating. It was also too expensive. In addition, the British didn't speak any of the Nigerian languages.

In 1900, Frederick Lugard became high commissioner for the region. He came up with an idea for allowing the Africans to govern themselves while still under his command. His plan was called *indirect rule*. It was based on the idea that all the people of Africa had a system of chiefs who already ruled their people, and that each group was separate from one another. Lugard was mistaken. All African people were not alike, and they did not all have the same kind of social structure

A royal salute on the King of England's birthday by British troops

The British had very little knowledge or understanding of these differences. Indirect rule worked best in the north, where the caliphs and emirs, the Muslim leaders, were willing to cooperate with the Europeans in order to maintain control over their own people. African people there were able to continue many of the laws that were important to them. In one area, though, they had to pay the price—the British expected their subjects (as they called the African people) to pay a tax for the privilege of being governed! The chiefs, whether they were called caliphs or emirs, kings or obas, were expected to collect this tax for the British. The chief was paid with some of the tax money that was collected.

Limiting Education

Lugard's actions in the north set the stage for the development of the region. Emirate rulers, who had religious and political authority, were highly opposed to Christian missionaries and western education. They insisted that the western missionaries be kept out.

Lugard prevented missionaries, who were already active in the south, from moving into the north. However, the missionaries were the main providers of education and medical help. As a result, the north began to lag behind the south. In the following decades, the two regions grew more and more apart. The Muslims kept a tight control over their people. Education, in Koran-based religious schools, and medical services were limited to what they could provide for themselves. They did not profit from advanced knowledge, especially in scientific development.

When Lugard's policy of indirect rule was brought to the south, the results were mixed. The Yoruba, who lived in the southwest, had well-established governments and traditional

Colonial administrators in Lagos meeting with messengers from the interior, 1910

kingdoms. Lugard's indirect rule was able to take advantage of these institutions. In the southeast, among the Igbo people, this was not possible. The Igbo did not have the same kind of government structures and were a much more independent people. There was a reason for this kind of independence. The land, filled with tropical swamps, made communication and travel extremely difficult. There was much more opposition to British attempts to introduce indirect rule.

In the north, the law of Islam, known as *sharia*, covered all court decisions about daily life, including disputes over land and requests for divorce. The government was conducted according to British ideas, but it was carried out by the emirs. This gave the north a sense of greater control than existed in the south. In many ways, northern and southern Nigeria were virtually two separate countries.

Slavery, which had provided so much wealth to some African leaders, was being ended. There was one unexpected drawback to this. The slaves had done most of the hard work in growing crops. When the slaves were freed, this labor source was lost and the economies were hard hit.

Merging North and South

As World War I (1914–1918) was beginning in Europe, Great Britain united the northern and southern protectorates. The Nigeria Council brought together six traditional leaders who were to speak for all the different regions of the colony.

With the war in Europe raging, the major European powers were more concerned with fighting one another than with conquering Africa. They began to use their new African colonies as part of the war effort. In Nigeria, Africans were recruited to take part in the war, both as soldiers and as laborers. Some Nigerians wound up fighting against other Africans in neighboring Cameroon, which was ruled by Germany. The war in Europe was now an African problem, too. After Germany lost the war, Great Britain added part of German Cameroon to its Nigeria colony.

In 1918, Lugard ended his control of Nigeria. Hugh Clifford took his place and supervised the colony until 1925. Clifford had very different ideas from Lugard. Because the north was so separate in its thinking, he felt it should be split off into a separate colony. Under Clifford's rule, the south began to have direct elections to a new, British-controlled legislative council. The people were getting a chance to participate in governing themselves again, as they had before the British arrived. The north, however, continued under the old rules.

African-American women, followers of Marcus Garvey, march in New York City, 1924.

First Steps toward Independence

Before long, a group of nationalists, people who wanted to create a country that was independent of Britain, began to form. They took their ideas from many sources, including the African-American movement in the United States. They admired the ideas of Marcus Garvey and W. E. B. Du Bois. At the same time, Nigerian Christian churches continued to mix local traditional religious practices into their services. In addition to being places of worship, the churches became meeting grounds where Nigerians could exchange ideas about nationalism

First Nigerian Political Movement

In 1923, the Nigerian National Democratic Party was formed by Herbert Macauley, who is often called the "father" of Nigerian nationalism. Macauley's movement took its main support from a small group of well-educated Africans in Lagos, the largest city. They soon realized that only a Nigeria completely free of the British would allow them to determine their own futures. In 1938, the Nigerian Youth Movement called for self-government. The British ignored this plea—but it was the first real rumbling of a move toward independence.

World War II

When the British found themselves caught up in World War II (1939–1945), they turned to the Nigerians again for help. About 100,000 Nigerians served on the British side during the war. Many Nigerian soldiers wondered why they were fighting to help the British resist domination, when they themselves had neither independence nor equality.

At this time, a spirit of freedom was growing around the world. The British found themselves giving up a number of their colonies in Asia. Many other colonies in Africa were also pushing to be independent of colonial rulers. The British slowly began a transition to Nigerian self-government.

Tafawa Balewa

They were realizing that they could no longer control the colony they had created.

The British government passed a Constitution for Nigeria in 1946. It gave the regional governments important powers. It established law-making houses of assembly in the three regions and reflected the differences among the three regions. While the Constitution was realistic, it actually kept Nigerians from becoming united. Forcing the regions to act as one nation was a recipe for ongoing struggle.

In the early 1950s, Nigerians won more rights and responsibilities. In the end, the groups agreed on at least one issue—they wanted independence from Great Britain. In 1959, a federal election was held, and on October 1, 1960, Nigeria became an independent country. Its prime minister was Tafawa Balewa. Benjamin Nnamdi Azikiwe, who was educated in the United States, became the governor-general. That position later was changed to president when Nigeria became a republic in 1963.

Fighting to Rule Nigeria

Now, Nigerians had every reason to believe that their country's future was bright. They had a parliamentary system of government, similar to that in Great Britain. Their leaders were elected for five-year terms. The framework of a modern democracy was in place.

Unfortunately, Nigeria was a nation in name only. Each region wanted to be governed in a way that benefited its own people. The people educated in the mission schools had a completely different outlook from those taught in Muslim schools. The emirs discouraged political change and kept decision making out of the hands of most of the people. Muslims didn't allow their women to vote.

Prime Minister Tafawa Balewa (second from right) at independence ceremony in 1960

New political parties developed in each of the regions. These were the Northern People's Congress (NPC), the western region's Action Group (AG), and the Ibos' group, the National Council of Nigeria and the Cameroons (NCNC).

The NPC tried to expand its power to include the south, especially seeking out those Yoruba who were Muslim. Yoruba leaders fought against the fraud and violence they found in the NPC. The southern parties were opposed to the political ideas of the conservative north, which followed Islamic ideas.

Differences among the regions now became major roadblocks to democracy. The north had control of the political situation, but it was much poorer than the south. Under Muslim rule, women were not allowed to take part in much of the life outside their homes. The north was the only region where women had not been allowed to vote.

Counting Heads

In 1963, the government set out to complete a census. This was necessary in order to determine the number of parliamentary seats each region would have. It also determined how much money the government should spend to develop each region.

People in the southeast and southwest regions did not believe that Nigeria's largest population lived in the north. When the census was counted, many people were furious. Areas in the east and west claimed their populations had grown at an enormous rate—more than twice as much as the north's. The north evened up the results by suddenly finding millions of "people" who hadn't been counted. In nearly forty years since then, there has never been an accurate count of the people in Nigeria or one that has been accepted by the Nigerians.

Military Takeovers

Within a few years of the 1963 census, Nigeria experienced its first military takeover. Soon after an election, a group of soldiers decided that the government should be run a different way. Some Nigerians thought that there had been cheating in counting the votes. On January 14, 1966, the military killed all three of the men fighting to gain control over the country. This takeover marked the beginning of a pattern—elections followed by military takeovers—that continued until 1999. The list of Nigeria's governments shows who was the head of the government during each period, and also the brief times when the country was a republic under civilian rule.

Governments since Independence

Years in power	Name of leader	Republic/Military rule
1960–1966	Tafawa Balewa	Republic
1966	J.T.U. Aguiyi-Ironsi	Military
1966–1975	Yakubu Gowon	Military
1975–1976	Murtala Mohammed	Military
1976–1979	Olusegun Obasanjo	Military
1979–1983	Shehu Shagari	Republic
1984–1985	Muhammadu Buhari	Military
1985–1993	Ibrahim Babangida	Military
1993–1998	Sani Abacha	Military
1998–1999	Abdulsalmi Abubakar	Military
1999–	Olusegun Obasanjo	Republic

Yakubu Gowon (third from right) holds a press conference in 1966.

Violence and the Military

After the first takeover, the military promised that the country would be returned to civilian rule. Riots and fighting broke out every time a new plan was announced to change the way the regions were represented.

Many of the officials were Igbo and were violent in their desire to support their own people. As soon as the military leader, Major General J.T.U. Aguiyi-Ironsi, announced his plan for a new government that would centralize power, the people of the north rioted. They saw the plan as proof that the general wanted to put the Igbo people in control of the entire country. Thousands of Igbo people were killed—the number is unknown.

More talks, more plans, and more rioting followed, as well as many more deaths. One million Igbo, who were living outside their region, fled home to the eastern region. In 1966, the military killed Ironsi and installed another military man, Lieutenant Colonel Yakubu Gowon, who ruled for nine years. At the beginning of his reign, Igbo leaders began to demand a separate state, to protect them from the northerners.

Instead, Gowon proposed a nation with twelve states. He wanted to make sure that the north was not the dominant region. He also wanted to give ethnic minorities representation. Additionally, Gowon wanted to make sure that control of the new, valuable oil fields located in the Igbo people's territory, would belong to the government.

In response to Gowan's plan, the governor of the eastern region announced it was seceding, or separating, from Nigeria. The region would now be an independent republic called Biafra. The name came from the Bight of Biafra, a body of water next to Igbo territory. The government responded swiftly and forcefully. A civil war began.

Biafra

Both sides had modern weapons. The government threw tremendous numbers of soldiers into the battle against the Biafrans. Although the government army had only 10,000 men in uniform at the beginning of the war, the army grew to nearly 250,000 soldiers by the end. The government set up a blockade to keep food and other supplies from entering Biafra,

Biafran soldiers with rifles aboard army boats

A starving Biafran family during the Biafran war

which led to widespread famine and disease in Biafra. Britain sided with the Nigerian government. Some other nations tried to support the Biafrans by breaking the blockade and bringing in vital supplies.

After two and a half years of fighting, the war ended in January 1970. By that time, hundreds of thousands of Igbo people had died from the fighting, but the number of people who died from disease and famine was well over 1 million and may have been as high as 3 million.

When the war ended, 3 million Igbo were refugees on a tiny piece of land. This was a time when Nigeria was beginning to gain tremendous profits from its oil reserves. The government used some of this money to rebuild the devastated region where the Igbo lived.

Obasanjo as Military Leader

Military regimes continued to follow one another, until Lieutenant General Olusegun Obasanjo was put into power by his fellow officers in 1976. Obasanjo was rare among the military leaders. He made real preparations for Nigeria to be returned to democratic civilian rule, including writing a new Constitution.

Up until this time, Nigeria's government was a parliamentary system, like that of Great Britain. The new Constitution changed the government to a presidential system, which took its example from the United States. To give more of the ethnic groups their own piece of land with their own capital and governor, the government increased the number of states in Nigeria to nineteen. Three years after Obasanjo came into power, he stepped down, in favor of a democratically elected president.

Unfortunately, bribery among the ministers of the new government was common. The people were outraged over the lack of honesty. It seemed to be no improvement over the military regimes that had come before.

The situation was made even worse by the collapse in the price paid for oil on world markets. Oil now accounted for more than 90 percent of the money earned for any product sold outside the country. Without this money, the government could not pay government employees or finish the development projects it had started. Politicians continued to steal money, not worrying about the future of the country. They started huge projects that they knew they couldn't pay for. In the process, they rolled up a huge amount of debt, leaving Nigeria's economy in sad shape.

Rigged Elections

The people running the country had become so used to doing things illegally that they didn't even care if the citizens could see them doing it. The results of the next elections, in 1983, were totally fraudulent. Officials counted people who didn't exist and gave certain candidates huge, and impossible, victories. The corruption was widespread. Once again, the military took over.

Several military leaders followed one another, each one being thrown out of office by the next. In 1985, General Ibrahim Babangida took over, taking the title of president. He managed to stay in office until 1993. He made some efforts to return the country to civilian rule, but he still held on to power very closely. In August 1991, he increased the number of states to thirty in another attempt to ease ethnic tensions.

Moshood K. O. Abiola was a political prisoner in Nigeria after being elected president.

Amazingly, one elected president doesn't even appear on the list of heads of government: Moshood K. O. Abiola. Although Abiola clearly won the election in 1993, two people stopped him from taking office. First, General Babangida, the military leader, threw out the election results. Then, when Abiola insisted on claiming his presidency, the man who followed Babangida, military leader Sani Abacha, had Abiola arrested and thrown in jail. Abiola was finally released in June 1998, but died one month later of a heart attack. Preventing Abiola from taking office deprived Nigeria of a remarkable man, one who began as the poorest of the poor. He succeeded in business and was well known for supporting many causes with his own money.

After the death of Sani Abacha, the country faced another election, and the prospects were not too promising. Most of the political parties had ties to former leaders including Abacha. Surprisingly, the former military leader, Olusegun Obasanjo was elected, this time as a civilian leader. There were charges of fraud on all sides of the election—in some places the voting polls never opened because the officials brought ballots to the voting stations that had already been filled out! However, Nigerians accepted the results. On May 29, 1999, Obasanjo took office.

Sani Abacha

Sani Abacha proved to be the worst leader Nigeria had ever known. He was more corrupt than all the leaders who had come before him, and he was more vicious in exercising power. During his five years in power, he stole billions of dollars from the oil industry and other sources. He put Nigeria completely in debt. During his reign, the income from oil that was reported by the Nigerian National Petroleum Company, the official government agency controlling oil production, was U.S.$2.7 billion less than the amount actually earned. Abacha stole the money and sent it to banks in Switzerland and other countries, to the accounts of his family and friends. The stolen money represented 10 percent of all the money earned in Nigeria. He died from a heart attack in June 1998.

CHAPTER

FIVE

Ruling Nigeria

NIGERIA'S NEW CIVILIAN GOVERNMENT ENACTED A NEW Constitution in 1999. Many aspects of the government are still being formed as the country returns to civilian rule. Now, Nigeria has thirty-six states and a new capital, Abuja.

In addition to the national government, there are 449 local governments. The government takes its structure from the Constitution of the United States. There are three branches of government—executive, legislative, and judicial.

Opposite: **Skyline of Abuja, Nigeria's new capital**

The Executive Branch

The president of Nigeria is the head of the executive branch. He is also commander-in-chief of the armed forces. The Federal Executive Council is made up of the president and ministers. The executive branch determines the policies and programs of the government. It also sees that the laws are carried out.

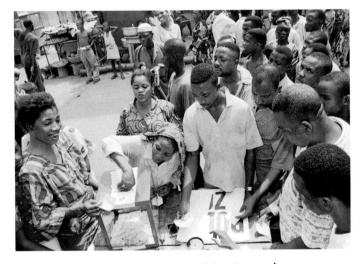

Nigerians gather to vote.

The president is elected directly by the people. He may be elected to no more than two four-year terms. He may not be a member of the National Assembly. He may not declare war. He appoints judges, but he can't remove them. The vice president is second in command.

NATIONAL GOVERNMENT OF NIGERIA

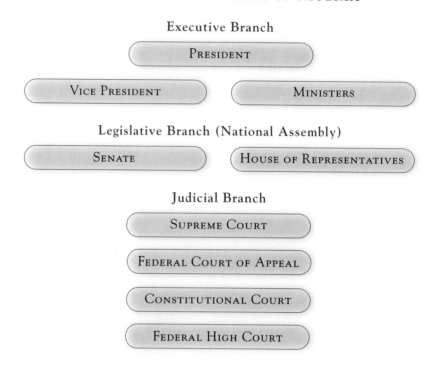

Executive Branch

PRESIDENT

VICE PRESIDENT   MINISTERS

Legislative Branch (National Assembly)

SENATE   HOUSE OF REPRESENTATIVES

Judicial Branch

SUPREME COURT

FEDERAL COURT OF APPEAL

CONSTITUTIONAL COURT

FEDERAL HIGH COURT

The Legislative Branch

The legislature, called the National Assembly, has two branches. The Senate has 109 members, 3 each from the thirty-six states, plus 1 to represent Abuja, the Federal Capital Territory. The House of Representatives has 360 members, elected by popular vote. Members of both the House and Senate are elected for seven-year terms.

The National Assembly makes the laws of the nation. It also has the very important power of amending, or changing, the Constitution.

The Senate president is third in power in the nation, after the president and the vice president. He presides over joint

Abuja: Did You Know This?

In the 1970s, the Nigerian government decided to build a new capital in the center of the country. This plan was meant to give Nigeria a new start in a place where there was no corruption. Construction of the capital began in the 1980s, but work went very slowly because money from oil had declined dramatically. The city grew very, very slowly. The government moved to Abuja even more slowly. Officials didn't want to leave lively Lagos, West Africa's largest city. Abuja is 310 miles (500 km) northeast of Lagos.

Population: 339,100 (1995)

Became capital: 1991

Altitude: 1,180 feet (360 m) above sea level

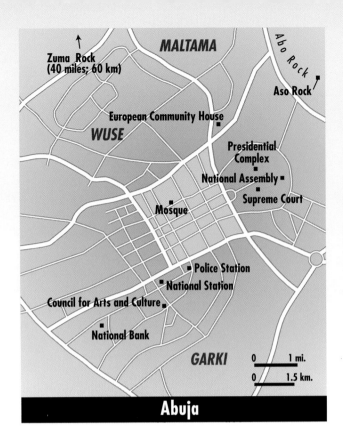

meetings of the National Assembly. The powers of the National Assembly may be challenged by the courts of the judicial branch.

The Judicial Branch

The judicial branch of government is headed by a Supreme Court with judges appointed by the Provisional Ruling Council. The Supreme Court is the highest court. It is headed by the chief justice, who serves with any number of justices as decided by an act of the National Assembly.

There is also a Federal Court of Appeal. Judges are appointed to it by the federal government. The Court of Appeal hears appeals from the other, lower courts of the nation.

The Constitutional Court is headed by a president and at least twenty justices. It interprets the Constitution. The Federal High Court presides over civil cases and financial matters of the government.

The High Court of the Federal Capital Territory (Abuja) consists of a chief judge and any number of other judges. It hears cases relating to civil and criminal proceedings in the Federal Territory. Other courts of the Federal Capital Territory are the Sharia Court of Appeal, which handles civil matters relating to Islamic law, and the Customary Court of Appeal, which handles civil matters relating to traditional law. Then there are state courts, including thirty-six high courts, one for each state, headed by a chief judge. These courts can hear any civil or criminal case.

Political Parties

Political parties, which were not permitted by the military government, were only allowed to start forming in July 1998. The ideas of competing peacefully to rule the country and working in a cooperative way in government are very new in

The Flag

Nigeria's national flag has three broad bars of equal size. The two green bars on either side represent agriculture. The white bar in the center represents peace and unity. The flag was first flown on October 1, 1960. A competition was held across Nigeria, and the winning design came from Michael Taiwo Akinkunmi, a student from the city of Ibadan.

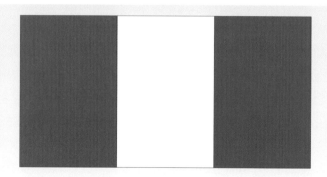

Olusegun Obasanjo

In a country where corruption has become common-place, President Olusegun Obasanjo stands out for his honesty. When he was elected in 1999, he immediately set out to repair all the horrors that had been Nigeria's history since independence.

Obasanjo is a Yoruba, born near Lagos. Before he joined the army, he was a schoolteacher. He was a military leader during the civil war in Biafra and led his division to a major victory over the Igbo rebels. That experience showed his ability to exercise power. It also gave him the support of the Muslims in the north, the home of most of Nigeria's military rulers. They supported him in spite of his being a Christian, brought up as a Baptist. Typical of the Yoruba, he has a farm in the countryside, where he raises pigs and chickens

Nigeria. The world is watching to see if this government, with this president, can manage to pull it off. Nigeria's future certainly depends on it.

CHAPTER

SIX

Wealth for
a Few

68

NIGERIA IS A COUNTRY THAT IS LITERALLY FLOATING IN oil and the wealth it brings. Even with all that money, the country's history has doomed it to be labeled as one of the poorest in the world. In reality, there are some extremely wealthy people in Nigeria, but most of the people have not profited from oil money.

Opposite: **A boy in Lagos with a hand-woven basket on his head**

Fetching water in a neighborhood of Lagos

Women beg for money from motorists on a Kano street named for Sani Abacha.

Some of Nigeria's former rulers, such as Sani Abacha, looked upon the money earned by oil as their own private fund. Others saw it as a resource that would enable Nigeria to quickly modernize. Enormous numbers of projects were started, especially in creating universities that were free for all students. Road-building projects began and electrical facilities were built. Nigeria's major cities were built up quickly and a new capital, at Abuja, was built from the ground up. But while Nigeria has plenty of oil to pump, it has no control over the price of that oil. When the price of oil fell, the government suddenly found itself unable to complete many projects. This happened in 1981–1982 and again in 1986.

The money flowed out faster than the oil could be pumped. A certain mentality developed in which officials demanded special bonuses, or bribes, just for doing their jobs. Sadly for Nigeria, living standards actually went down after oil was discovered.

Ken Saro-Wiwa

When author Ken Saro-Wiwa and eight other men were executed on November 10, 1995, shock waves were felt around the world. They were killed because of their involvement in the cause of the Ogoni people in the Niger Delta. Saro-Wiwa was a member of a small tribe, the Khana, who were grouped together with the Ogonis by the government. He saw the extreme poverty of his people and the way they were neglected throughout Nigerian history. He wanted the Ogoni people to share in the enormous profits that were being made in their homeland. He also saw the terrible pollution created by oil drilling that threatened the people's health.

Saro-Wiwa wrote a number of books including *Songs in a Time of War*, *Sozaboy*, and *A Forest of Flowers*. He even wrote a Nigerian comedy that poked fun at people who represented well-known characters in Nigeria. However, his political activities gave him the most public exposure and ultimately led to his death. The outrage over his death had some immediate results. Thirty countries withdrew their ambassadors to protest against the Abacha government, which had ordered the trial and death of Saro-Wiwa and others convicted with him. That was a sign of extreme international anger.

Yet for Saro-Wiwa's people, nothing has changed. Though his family managed to give him a funeral, it was five years after he died. His parents live in extreme poverty, like most of the people in the region. They don't have clean water to drink, electricity, or even a decent road. The wealth of the region's oil still doesn't reach the half-million Ogoni people. In 2000, the new government decided that more money should be directed to the Delta Region. It increased the amount of money the nine oil-producing states receive to 13 percent of the money earned from oil. This is a huge amount of money. In just three months, the government gave the states more than U.S.$1 billion dollars.

Farming Declines

One of the other effects of Nigeria's oil wealth has been to discourage farmers from growing crops. In 1960, at the time of independence, Nigeria's three main agricultural products—cocoa, peanuts, and palm oil—produced 70 percent of its export earnings. Twenty years later, food exports, mainly cocoa, accounted for only 3 percent of exports. By 1985, Nigeria had largely given up on producing its own food and had to import peanuts and cooking oil.

Pyramids of sacks containing peanuts in Kano

What Nigeria Grows, Makes, and Mines

Agriculture (1996)

Yams	23,640,000 metric tons
Cassava	21,000,000 metric tons
Corn (maize)	7,321,000 metric tons

Manufacturing (1990, valued added in U.S.$)

Food and beverages	$703,000,000
Textiles	$373,000,000
Chemical products	$165,000,000

Mining (1994)

Petroleum	665,994,000 barrels
Limestone	2,700,000 metric tons
Marble (1992)	30,661 metric tons
Tin	300 metric tons

The Sweet Crop

Cocoa (or cacao) was introduced by the British, who wanted to turn their new colony into a money-making operation. Unlike farm crops such as yams that were grown for food, cocoa was grown only to be sold. Cocoa beans are the principal ingredient in chocolate. Chocolate candy bars, chocolate ice cream, and all chocolate treats start with cocoa beans.

Nigeria was one of the major producers of cocoa in the world through the 1970s, growing an average of 400,000 tons of beans each year. But farmers needed help from the government to transport their crops to market. When the government began to focus almost exclusively on money earned from oil, farming was neglected. Many farmers gave up growing cocoa beans. The yearly output of cocoa declined to 135,000 tons.

Now, the crop is once more being grown. Many people who had left their farms for the big cities, particularly Lagos and Ibadan, discovered there wasn't enough work for them. They have returned to the farms and have contributed to a huge increase in production. The government has big plans for cocoa—in 2000, it distributed 892,000 cocoa seedlings to farmers. The goal is to produce more than 1 million tons of cocoa a year. Cocoa-tree farming is concentrated in the south-western area where the Yoruba live.

Worker planting cocoa seeds

Nigerian Money

The basic unit of currency in Nigeria is the *naira*. Each naira is divided into 100 *kobo*, although the value of the kobo is so small that it is rarely used. The bills feature important figures from Nigeria's history, women doing farm work, and musicians playing instruments.

Nigeria is considering a plan to join with five other English-speaking West African countries to create a single currency that they would all use. This plan is similar to the recent changeover in Europe, where many countries are giving up their national currencies in favor of the new currency, the euro.

Oil Is King

Every single day, more than 2 million barrels of oil are produced by Nigeria's oil wells. Oil is Nigeria's most important product. It accounts for about 95 percent of the country's entire exports and most of the country's income. Each barrel of oil sells for about U.S.$25–U.S.$30 at current prices. Of course, that is not all profit, but it still creates an annual income of about U.S.$10 billion. Oil companies must pay taxes to the Nigerian government in order to operate in the country. The oil companies also pay Nigeria for permission to drill for oil.

The biggest oil producing company in Nigeria is Royal Dutch/Shell, a company based in the Netherlands. This company began exploring for oil in Nigeria in 1937, but it wasn't

Workers at an oil company near Port Harcourt

until 1956 that the first commercial oil field was found. The company once pumped 6,000 barrels of oil a day. It now produces about half of all the oil pumped in Nigeria. Other major companies are Chevron, Elf, Texaco, and Agip.

The oil is pumped out of the ground at the oil fields, which are found throughout the Niger Delta. Once in the pipeline, oil goes either to a refinery or to a tanker waiting offshore. Supertankers can carry 200,000 metric tons. Oil tankers then carry millions of gallons of oil to refineries around the world. The United States is one of the major buyers of Nigeria's oil.

A girl carrying greens walks past a row of oil pipes.

While oil tankers sometimes run into trouble and create huge oil spills in the oceans, this has not been a problem for Nigeria. The problem here starts before the oil ever reaches the tankers. In Nigeria, about 3,000 miles (5,000 km) of pipelines crisscross the Niger Delta, cutting across fields and farmland. These pipelines may leak and spill oil. Oil spills harm plants, animals, land, and people.

In the past, oil companies didn't pay much attention to these spills. They usually gave money to the local chief to pay for damages to the land. However, this money rarely took care of the farmers whose land had been spoiled.

Many people were furious that oil flowed over their land, but they didn't receive benefits from it. Over the years, they have taken matters into their own hands. They have actually punched holes in the pipelines that carry gasoline between the delta and northern Nigeria. The people rush in to scoop

In the Niger Delta near Warri, workers clean up an oil spill caused by vandals.

A girl flees a pipeline fire that started after leaking gasoline exploded.

up the gasoline in buckets or bowls. Then they sell the gasoline, usually to other people who have organized this illegal activity into a big business.

Because gasoline bursts into flames very easily, tragedies sometimes occur. The most recent was a series of fires that erupted in the Niger Delta after a gasoline pipeline exploded. More than 700 people were killed and many others were horribly burned. Farmland and homes in the area were destroyed.

Because most of the world needs oil and petroleum products, you might think that Nigeria is a wealthy nation. The money has not made its way to the average Nigerian citizen, and it has especially not made its way to the people who live right in the oil producing region, the Ogoni people. They have

No Gas at the Pumps

There is a shortage of gasoline in Nigeria even though the country seems to have plenty of oil. In order to bring gasoline, which comes from oil, to the pumps at the local filling station, oil must be refined. Nigeria had four major refineries to take care of its own oil needs. But during the years of military governments, these refineries were not maintained and were allowed to deteriorate. The military governments needed oil but they liked money better. They allowed other countries to sell the government-refined oil as long as they received part of the fee. By the time the last military rule had ended, Nigeria found itself in the ridiculous situation of being a major oil producer with no gas at its own pumps.

been protesting against the oil companies for years. Their most prominent spokesperson was Ken Saro-Wiwa.

Now, the government is getting even more money from oil, and the oil hasn't even been pumped! More oil has been discovered undersea off the Nigerian coastline. Oil companies bid as much as U.S.$200 million just for the right to pump this oil. They expect to make billions from it, once the pumping actually begins. Offshore oil has tremendous advantages for companies—from undersea, the oil is pumped directly into tankers. It does not come into contact with the land or the people living there. Another 1 million barrels a day could come from these offshore oil fields.

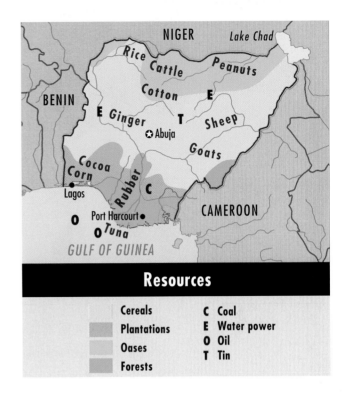

Resources

	Cereals	C	Coal
	Plantations	E	Water power
	Oases	O	Oil
	Forests	T	Tin

An oil rig in the shallow waters along the coast

General Sani Abacha

Thanks to its oil production, Nigeria has been earning billions of dollars every year from taxes and mining royalties, paid by the foreign-owned oil companies. Yet the country is so short of money that it has not been able to repair roads, keep the electric lights on, or even see that enough gasoline reaches its own filling stations.

Where did all the money go? Former president Sani Abacha stole U.S.$2–3 billion. He hid it in bank accounts in Europe. In 2000, the government of Nigeria was beginning to get some of that money back. A "down payment" of U.S.$66 million was returned to the central Nigerian bank by a Swiss bank in July 2000. It was just the beginning of what President Obasanjo hopes to reclaim.

Mining

Long before oil was discovered, Nigeria was known for producing tin, an important mineral. Tin has many uses. For example, a thin coating of tin is used on many kinds of food containers, such as soft drink cans. Since 1920, Amalgamated Tin Mines of Bukuru has mined tin on the Jos Plateau, far to the north of Lagos. Workers operated an enormous machine that could scoop up tons of ore at once.

In the 1970s, 10,000 tons of tin ore were produced every year. The ore was processed right at the mine, washed in long wooden containers called sluices. It was dirty, messy work, but it was the main source of income for men of the region. Production dropped in the 1980s and by the 1990s had slowed to 500 tons a year

Mining became more expensive as the deposits were used up. The miners had to dig deeper and deeper to bring up the ore. In the process, they had to destroy more of the land, leaving huge pits. Nigeria was once the sixth most important producer of tin in the world. Now it is a minor producer.

The country also has very large deposits of iron ore, and mining of these is underway. Its forest reserves are a tiny fraction of what they were 100 years ago.

Production has fallen for tin mining.

Speaking of
Nigerians

THERE IS NO LANGUAGE CALLED NIGERIAN AND THERE IS no ethnic group known as Nigerian. A Nigerian is someone who lives in the nation of Nigeria. There are many ethnic groups in the country, and most people identify themselves as members of these groups. The largest groups are the Hausa-Fulani (30–35 percent), the Yoruba (20–25 percent), and the Igbo (18–20 percent). Igbo is also spelled *Ibo* because the "g" is not pronounced.

People may also be identified as members of a particular religious group. Muslims in the north, in particular, have chosen recently to govern themselves by the laws of their religion, setting themselves apart from their Christian neighbors. People also identify themselves by the language, or languages, they speak.

Opposite: **A woman selling roasted ears of maize in a Lagos market**

An ornamental ivory mask once worn by a Benin king

Benin Culture

The Benin culture is best known today for its amazing bronze castings. The leader of the Benin, called the *oba*, was much more important in the lives of his people than even a king would be today. He ruled them culturally, spiritually, and politically. All works of art were made in his honor. During the 1500s and 1600s—more than 400 years ago—the Benin were creating fine masks in ivory. These very detailed masks had idealized features; that is, they represented the best face the sculptor could create.

The Benin kingdom, which began as a small collection of villages around the twelfth century, was at the height of its power in the 1400s. A very powerful oba, Ewuare, formed an

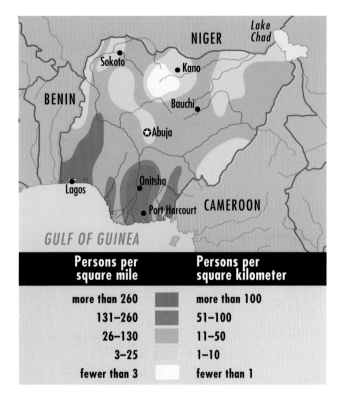

Persons per square mile		Persons per square kilometer
more than 260		more than 100
131–260		51–100
26–130		11–50
3–25		1–10
fewer than 3		fewer than 1

Who Lives in Nigeria?

Hausa	21%
Yoruba	21%
Igbo (Ibo)	18%
Fulani	11%
Ibibio	6%
Kanuri	4%
Edo	3%
Tiv	2%
Ijaw	2%
Bura	2%
Nupe	1%
Other	9%

army and conquered surrounding villages. The kingdom grew not only in size, but in the quality of life. The oba set up a system of law and a city that was as modern and well kept as European cities of the time. The city's wealth came from its art, pepper, leopard skins, and eventually, the slave trade.

Slavery proved to be Benin's downfall. As the slave trade grew, trade in agricultural products was ignored. Money was spent on wars among Benin and other slave-trading kingdoms. Just a few hundred years after Ewuare came to power, the kingdom was back to being just a collection of little villages.

The Hausa

The Hausa, who live in the far north of the country, have very different lives from the people who live in the south. The Hausa language is the most widely spoken language in Nigeria. It was an official language in the north during the 1960s, which helped to spread its use beyond the Hausa people themselves. Historically, the Hausa lived along the trade routes coming across the Sahara, which brought not only new materials but also new ideas. The Hausa are known for their skill in trading, perhaps because they were at the center of the trade routes. Goods were exchanged in Kano, the major Hausa city, and sent out on caravans.

The Muslim religion is at the heart of Hausa culture, and it influences virtually every aspect of daily life. Schools teach children how to be good Muslims by following the Koran, the Muslim holy book. School is at the center of Hausa life. Although at one time the Hausa were considered the most modern thinkers, this is not the case today. Emphasis on learning from the Koran has limited their advances in scientific and technical areas and has also ruled out much learning from Western sources.

Vendors sell bowls and cooking pots at a market in Kano.

The Yoruba

The Yoruba are an ancient people who live in southwestern Nigeria. Their history began between the eleventh and the fifteenth centuries, when their ancestors lived in the kingdom of Ile-Ife. Here, the Yoruba believe Earth itself was created.

Recently, scientists discovered the ruins of an ancient wall, 100 miles (160 km) long and surrounded by a moat, in the ancient Yoruba kingdom. It is thought the wall took more than 300 years to build. As it is studied, it will provide more clues to the origins of the Yoruba people.

Population of Nigeria's Largest Cities (2001 est.)	
Lagos	8–13,000,000
Ibadan	5,000,000
Kano	1,000,000
Ogbomosho	800,000
Oshogbo	500,000
Enugu	500,000

Yoruba men wear *agbadas*, long, loose robes.

The Yoruba have their own gods, which number in the hundreds. Four of their gods are very important. These are Sango, the god of thunder and lightning; Ifa, the god of divination, who tells the future; Eshu, the trickster; and Ogun, the god of war.

Today, the Yoruba are both city dwellers and farmers. They have lived in large cities for centuries, following their trading traditions. They also keep farms in the rural areas, where they grow yams and cassava, two basic foods. Lagos and Ibadan, the two largest cities in Nigeria, are known as Yoruba cities because most of the people are from this ethnic group. Because of their close connection with city life, the Yoruba have better opportunities for education and for business.

Nigerian Words

Like other people who speak English, Nigerians have invented local words to describe things from everyday life. These words may be taken directly from English and used diffeently, or they may be words from one of the local languages that are used along with English. Here are some examples.

buka	a cheap restaurant in a shack
don	used as the past tense (for example, "I don shop.")
el hadjis	rich businessmen
go	used as the future tense (for example, "I go shop.")
hear	used to mean "speak" (for example, "I hear Hausa.")
kiss	when a car bumps into another car
moto	car (taken from "motor")

Yoruba Beadwork

The Yoruba believe the obas, who number about 700, are direct descendants of the god Oduduwa. The Yoruba obas wear beautiful robes and headdresses that are covered in elaborate and complex beadwork. Every object made for an oba is beaded, from his slippers to the crown.

The crowns are especially important because they represent the authority of the obas. The crowns have beaded birds—called okins—perched on them. This royal bird looks as if it is about to fly away. The crown also has a fringe of beads to hide the oba's identity.

Yams are the staple food of the Yoruba, so they celebrate a successful harvest with great ceremony. The Yoruba make long, beaded banners for the occasion. The beaded banners also feature the okin bird and a pattern called *salubata*, which is a series of interwoven S shapes. The endless pattern represents the eternal quality of the Yoruba people.

The Igbo

Of all the major ethnic groups in Nigeria, the Igbo are the only ones who did not develop a system of kings or monarchies. They had a large population, governed in small, democratically run villages. Each person took part in making village decisions.

The Igbo are among the most competitive people in Nigeria, striving for success. In the nineteenth century, their large village groups had between 1,000 to 3,000 people in each. As the years went by, these villages grew. This increase in population made it difficult for the Igbo to continue to find enough farmland to grow food. Partly as a result, the Igbo have tended to migrate throughout Nigeria, and they form minority groups in most of the country's large cities. They are known as traders, and both men and women are often involved in business. Their competitive nature tends to make the Igbos outsiders among the other Nigerian peoples.

Role of Chiefs

For most Nigerians who live in the rural areas, in small villages and towns, a local chief governs daily life. The chief, known as the oba, caliph, or emir, has a major role to play in the life of his people. Chiefs do not hold public office, but by tradition they exert a very strong authority, and they are vital in maintaining the culture of their people. Although land ownership in some areas is simply a matter of buying and selling land, in other regions chiefs still control the right to use the land. The chief is also the spiritual leader of his people. He may tell the people when it is time to plant their crops.

A chief surrounded by people

Chiefs usually inherit their titles, or they may be chosen from among all the sons of a leader at his death. Some of the obas are well-educated men who have college degrees. However, many chiefs have little more education than the people they rule. They use their own experience and the information passed along from father to son to make decisions for their people.

Masked dancers

Masks

Throughout Africa, people make masks for ceremonies, which usually involve dancing. These masks can be made of wood or leather, and they are often decorated with real teeth, nails, hair, fur, and many other materials. Masks are usually made in secret and hidden away until they are used. When a dancer wears a mask, he or she seems to become someone else, a kind of spirit. Masks are used in the secret societies that still exist in parts of Nigeria, especially among the Igbo people. Masked dancers perform these rituals to keep the beliefs and stories of the culture alive, and to pass them on to the next generation

Benin Bronzes

From the fifteenth century until the end of the nineteenth century, Benin artists used bronze to create beautifully sculptured figures of Benin royalty. The kings or obas, were the only people who could commission a bronze casting. These castings showed the rituals, clothing, and ornaments used in sacred ceremonies.

Sometimes, more than fifty years would pass between coronations. It was only the bronzes that showed the correct way to dress for the occasion. They are the "written" history of the Benin people. The bronzes are considered religious objects, not simply works of art.

Masked dances are more than just entertainment. They are an important part of the cultural expression of the group. For example, in Igbo dances, the men act out warnings from the spirits that govern behavior and maintain the group's moral standards.

FESPAC

In 1977, a month-long cultural festival was staged in Nigeria, called the Festival of Pan-African Culture (FESPAC). More than 15,000 artists, musicians, writers, and dancers from all over the world gathered in Nigeria to celebrate African culture in its many forms.

The festival was a great showcase for Nigeria, which acted as the host nation. It was also a way of acknowledging the great art that has come from Nigeria. While Nigeria's cultural history was on display, the festival also highlighted contemporary work including filmmaking. Nigeria hoped to show that while their cultures are very different, the need for artistic expression is something shared by all people. It was a way to bring all these people together.

Lagos, The Go-Slow City

There are big cities, and then there is Lagos. This coastal city, for decades the capital of Nigeria, has an enormous population. Estimates range from 8 million up to 13 million people. The United Nations says that Lagos is the largest city in Africa, and the sixth most populous city in the world.

People live in a city famous around the world for its "go-slows," traffic that hardly inches along. The city has a modern business district full of skyscrapers, often with banks on the street level. There are middle-class neighborhoods with lovely homes and regions with homes that are truly mansions.

The geography of Lagos is as complicated as a maze because the city is built on four islands in a lagoon, and also on the mainland. Bridges connect all the parts of the city. Lagos is also Nigeria's main port. It is full of people and traffic and has been an important Yoruba city since the fifteenth century.

The city has grown much faster than its housing. As people flood into Lagos, looking for work, they build shacks from anything they find in the streets—cardboard, wood, pieces of metal, discards from other people. Many people live underneath the highways that connect the parts of the city. The city's big and busy Balogun Market is the place to go to buy just about everything.

Lagos is the most important city in Nigeria. It is the commercial center of the country, and the place to do business of all kinds. It is home to about 10 percent of the people of Nigeria.

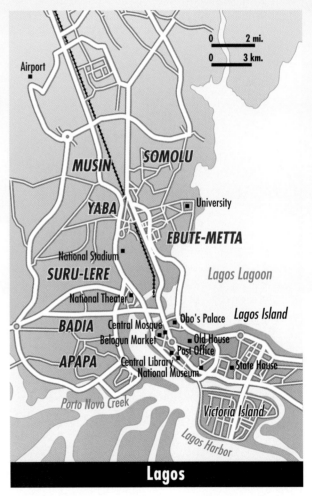

Religion
in Crisis

R ELIGION IS AN IMPORTANT PART OF THE DAILY LIVES OF almost all Nigerians. Three types of religious practices are found in Nigeria—Islam, Christianity, and traditional African religions. People often combine their beliefs, continuing with their traditional religion but joining it with Christian or Muslim beliefs. It is estimated that 50 percent of the people are Muslim, 40 percent are Christian, and 10 percent follow the traditional African religion.

In the region of Nigeria, before the coming of outside religions, the people followed traditional beliefs with ancient beginnings. The lives of people were tied closely to their ancestors through their religious beliefs. These beliefs were part of everyday life. Everyone in the community shared these beliefs. This is called *indigenous* religion.

Today, it is estimated that about 10 percent of the people still follow their indigenous religion. In practice, many people who are part of Muslim or Christian religions also continue to believe in their traditional religions.

One of the main differences between traditional beliefs and the Christian and Muslim religions is in the number of gods the people believe in. Followers of both the Christian and Muslim religions believe in one god, but people who follow traditional religions believe in many gods.

Opposite: **A mosque in Abuja welcomes Muslims to worship.**

Religions of Nigeria

Muslim	50%
Protestant	20%
Roman Catholic	20%
Traditional	10%

Important Religious Holidays

Id al-Fitr/Id al-Sighir	December or January
Tabaski/Id al-Kabir	February or March
Easter	A Sunday in March or April
Muslim New Year's Day	March or April
Ramadan	Ninth month (Islamic calendar)
Christmas	December 25

A traditional religious festival at Oshun River

Traditional Religion

Traditional African religion begins with a belief in one god who created Earth and the heavens. Religious practice involves paying a constant series of obligations to dead ancestors. The spirits of these ancestors are very real to the people.

Other spirits are thought to live in all natural things, including trees, rivers, animals, and rocks. Spirits can move from place to place. Living people have to take care of these spirits so they remain peaceful. These beliefs make the people very good caretakers of their land and natural resources. In return, the spirits bless the people and give them good crops and clean water to drink.

To protect themselves from bad or evil things, people wear charms and amulets. They take special potions, or medicines, prepared by members of their tribes who have special powers.

Islam

Islam, the Muslim religion, dominates the northern half of Nigeria. It was introduced by traders nearly 1,000 years ago. Islam moved quickly through the region in the next 500 years until it met resistance by local people who did not want to be ruled by the emirs.

The religion began in the year A.D. 610, in the Arabian Peninsula, when a merchant named Muhammad began to preach his vision about the god he called Allah. Muhammad is called the prophet of Allah—the one who spreads the message. From this beginning, the Muslim religion spread across the lands of the Arabs where it began, and then into Africa.

Praying outside a mosque in Kano

Muslim Practices

Muslims pray five times a day. When Muslims pray, they always face toward Mecca, Saudi Arabia, to honor the place where the religion began. They have five obligations—to state that there is no god but Allah and Muhammad is his prophet; to recite their daily prayers; to give charity to those in need; to fast at certain times of the year; and to make a pilgrimage to Mecca. These duties are carried out by everyone except the sick, the very young, and women who are pregnant or recently gave birth. The obligation to travel to Mecca once in a lifetime is considered a great honor. If a person cannot afford to make the trip, there is no shame attached to it.

The Muslim calendar is based on the lunar year, so the months occur in different seasons. Ramadan, a period of intense daily fasting and prayer, is the most solemn month. The end of Ramadan, which lasts four weeks, comes when the new moon is sighted.

In the Islamic religion, a man is permitted to have as many as four wives at one time, if he can afford them. He is obliged to treat them equally. While fewer men today have more than one wife, this practice still exists, especially among older people and chiefs in rural areas. Under traditional religion, the practice of having more than one wife continues as well.

Islam is so much a part of daily life among its followers that it is impossible to separate religious life from civil life. For this reason, anyone who lives in a Muslim area and who practices

Usman Dan Fodio

At the end of the eighteenth century, a Muslim teacher named Usman dan Fodio set about to change the way the people of the Hausa states lived their lives. He believed that the Hausa rulers were not following Islamic law. They forced the people to pay enormous taxes to finance their own governments.

Usman wanted to bring the people back to a more religious way of life. In order to force the Hausa rulers to change, he launched a holy war, known as a *jihad*. He and his followers conquered the whole region and built a new capital at Sokoto in 1809. Under his rule, the capital became known as the Sokoto caliphate, which is something like a religious kingdom.

Usman himself was not a Hausa, he was a Fulani, a much smaller group. Following his lead, most of the leaders of his time were Fulani. The Sokoto caliphate covered nearly all of Nigeria north of the Niger and Benue Rivers. It was the largest empire in Africa at that time. The jihad also inspired neighboring people to set up Islamic states that stretched across Africa.

Muslim and Christian women get into a public van.

a different religion lives a completely separate life. Christians, such as the Igbo, live in their own areas and cannot participate in many of the decisions that rule the area.

This separatism creates a wall between the people and keeps them from feeling they are part of the same nation. It also makes it impossible for many non-Muslims in the north to work in businesses or participate in politics. Both economic and political power is in the hands of Muslims.

The recent introduction of Islamic religious law, called *sharia*, into the northern states is putting a great strain on the people. Among the Muslims, many are very religious, while others prefer a more relaxed approach to religion. However, when a northern state in Nigeria declares that sharia is the official law covering all matters, both criminal and traditional, for all Muslims, the people have little choice about how they conduct their lives.

Christianity

Christian religions have had a much shorter history in Nigeria. Missionaries were kept out because of the climate and local diseases, especially malaria. Even as late as the mid-1840s, exploration of Nigeria's rivers was limited to a few bold adventurers.

A brief attempt to bring Christianity to the people took place at Benin in the fifteenth century when Portuguese Roman Catholic priests arrived with traders. They managed to build several churches and converted a small number of Africans to the religion.

The Portuguese presence was brief, and so was the Roman Catholic missionary movement. It began again, in a small area between Lagos and Ibadan in the 1840s. The Church of England sent its Missionary Society, and other Protestant groups soon followed from Great Britain, Canada, and the United States. Roman Catholic sects came in the 1860s. Each group remained in a particular area and, as a result, the Yoruba tended to be Protestant while the Igbo were Catholic.

Limiting Christianity

Missionary influence and Christianity did not travel far into Nigeria. Colonial high commissioner Frederick Lugard actively kept the missionaries from traveling to the north. He preferred to govern through the emirs, allowing them to settle many issues through their already established Islamic law courts, under the sharia system.

A girl reads passages from the Koran.

If the missionaries started converting people to Christianity, this balance would be upset. As a result, Lugard strengthened the importance of Islam in the north, further dividing the society into northern and southern regions. This approach also set the stage for the institution of Islamic schools whose teachings focused on the writings of the Koran, the Muslim holy book. Young Muslim children memorized parts of the Koran before they learned to read.

Christian Sects

From these beginnings, the people of the south were divided among Christian denominations. Yoruba follow Anglican and other Protestant churches. The Igbo people usually belong to a Roman Catholic church. In many cases, churches set up both schools and clinics, the only such facilities for the people.

However, European-style Christianity does not always sit well with many African people. Traditional African beliefs are at odds with many Christian rituals. One result has been the introduction of the Aladura church in the Yoruba area. *Aladura* means "people of prayer" in the Yoruba language. The movement began in the early twentieth century within the framework of the Anglican, Methodist, and Baptist churches.

Aladura is a religion with strong, charismatic leaders. *Charisma* is the ability to excite and lead people to follow your beliefs. There are many such churches now in Nigeria, and the movement has even reached Europe and the United States. Unlike more traditional Christian churches, the Aladura movement does not seek to convert others. It takes its strength from its leader rather than from a particular set of ideas. People follow this one leader—he or she really represents the church.

By combining Christian beliefs with traditional Yoruba religious practices, the Aladura church offers a comfortable place to worship for many Yoruba people. It focuses on healing and accepts the idea that people need to be protected from evil forces. The church even supports a tradition of polygamy—having more than one wife at a time—which is against traditional Christian beliefs.

Enforcing Islamic Law

Throughout most of Nigeria's history as an independent nation, the federal government has been ruled by Muslims from the north. The military governments, with one exception, have been headed by Muslims. That exception was Olusegun Obasanjo, a Yoruba and a Christian, who rules as president and who also was one of those military leaders. Barely a year after he was elected president, a movement began in the north that threatens to throw the country into violence and a possible return to military rule. It started in Kaduna, one of the northern states, and then spread rapidly across the north. It was the declaration that the Islamic law known as sharia was to be the law in these states in all criminal matters, not just in family and personal matters as was true before.

Against Nigerian Law

The Nigerian Constitution clearly states: "The government of the Federation or of a State shall not adopt any religion as State Religion." But that is exactly what is being done in many of the northern states of Nigeria. One after the other, the governors of those states declared sharia to be the only law, although it was only to be applied to Muslims. Some of these states, such as Yobe and Kaduna, have equal numbers of Muslims and Christians, but they have introduced sharia too.

How Sharia Differs

Sharia differs from civil law mainly in the kinds of punishments that are permitted. While certain actions such as theft are crimes under both kinds of law, sharia punishments tend to be physical. In civil law, the crime of theft might be punished by imprisonment. Under sharia, a thief may have his hand cut off. If he commits a second theft, he may have a foot cut off. Other actions, such as drinking alcohol and gambling, are only

Muslim and Christian girls line up at the start of a lesson at a secondary school for girls. Christian pupils wear their traditional headdress. Muslims wear the Islamic *hijab*.

crimes under Muslim law. Flogging—beating or striking with a stick or a leather strap—has been carried out for drinking alcohol, which is forbidden by the Koran.

Sharia goes further in separating men and women in public. Women have been forced to give up certain freedoms. In Zamfara, for example, where motorbikes are used as taxis, women have been forbidden to ride on the back of motorbikes even if their husbands are the drivers. Schools in the northern states are segregated by sex. In the south, boys and girls go to school together.

Why did the northern states choose to make sharia the law at this particular time? In Nigeria, nearly everything has its roots in politics. Because President Obasanjo is a Christian from the south, the religious leaders in the north may have seen this as a way of balancing the power in the country. As soon as the governor of one state adopted sharia, others followed. They were afraid that if they didn't, people would wonder if they were faithful enough to their religion.

Dividing the People

Two hundred people died in battles between Muslims and Christians in Kaduna when sharia was first introduced and the government was forced to call in army troops and riot police. There has been a flood of Christians leaving the region. Many had lived in the area for a long time and had businesses and homes. They suddenly found themselves in danger and left the area. The Igbo, especially, are afraid to stay in the north. Their memories of how the nation was torn apart by the civil war in 1967–1970 make them fear for their lives. The roads have been full of people leaving areas where they are the minority; the Christians are heading south, and the Muslims are moving north.

The new policy has also put a stop to one of Nigeria's most important projects aimed at bringing people together—the National Youth Service Corps. After the civil war in Biafra, the government wanted to heal wounds created by the war, and to bridge the gaps between the people living in different regions of the country. The government established the National Youth Service Corps. All college graduates, including those attending technical colleges, would spend one year working away from their home state. Students from the south were sent to the north; students from the north were sent to the south. After Kano and some of the other states in the north announced they were imposing sharia, the Christian Association of Nigeria announced it was halting the program. Parents were afraid to send their children to the north where civil laws were no longer followed.

By April 2001, ten northern states had introduced sharia as the law. Punishments became more severe. The problem threatens Nigeria's ability to continue as a nation.

Arts and Culture

For many centuries, Nigeria has had a rich artistic and musical culture. The tradition continues today, especially in music, writing, and art. Many Nigerian writers have reached worldwide audiences. This is partly because they write in English, but also because they tell fascinating stories that appeal to readers everywhere. Their talents have been recognized around the world.

In 1986, author Wole Soyinka won the Nobel Prize for Literature, the first African writer to earn this honor. He won for an entire body of work, more than twenty major pieces of playwriting. One of his first plays, *A Dance of the Forests*, was written just as Nigeria gained independence. It takes its story from the life of the times and the people, just as all his work does. Soyinka is an excellent example of a modern Nigerian: He is a Yoruba, raised as a Christian, who prefers traditional religion. He brings the Yoruba god, Ogun, to life in his writing. He angered Nigerian dictators for his attempts to improve life in his native country and was imprisoned for two years. Fearing for his life, he left Nigeria, and has lived abroad for some years.

Opposite: **Drummers on their way to a wedding**

Wole Soyinka now lives and teaches in the United States.

Ben Okri

Among Nigeria's other honored writers are Ben Okri and Chinua Achebe. Okri won the Booker Prize in 1991 for his novel *The Famished Road*. The novel tells a story that weaves in beliefs in the supernatural. Amos Tutuola was the earliest Nigerian author to become known outside the country. His novel *The Palm-Wine Drinkard* was published in 1952. It uses Yoruba myths and legends and focuses on a boy who drinks a great deal of palm wine, one of the country's major exports before independence.

Chinua Achebe

Things Fall Apart by Chinua Achebe may be the most famous novel to be written by a Nigerian. It has sold 8 million copies worldwide. It is a simple story about relationships over the years in a village, but it gives the reader a very detailed look at what it means to live a traditional life. The book was published just before Nigeria became independent, and there is no sense of the changes that are coming. Achebe lived through those changes, growing up while the British still ruled Nigeria as a colony. He has said that the truck that brought the mail, the Royal British Post, was the symbol of colonial authority in his village.

For many years, Achebe has lived in the United States. An automobile accident in Lagos's notorious traffic left him paralyzed from the waist down. He came to the United States for medical treatment, something he felt was not available at home. Now confined to a wheelchair, he feels he is better able to get around in a country where disabled people have strong rights and where facilities accommodate their needs.

Nigerian music has led the way in West Africa for a long time. It has a wonderful, toe-tapping quality whether it is the music known as highlife, the juju music of King Sunny Ade, or the Afro-beat music started by Fela Kuti.

Musician King Sunny Ade playing in a concert

Traditional African drums come in an enormous variety of types, sizes, and sounds and are used to create very complicated rhythms. Many different rhythms are played at the same time, with the melodies woven around the beats. Nigerian singers have recorded music that reaches around the world.

Juju music began in the 1920s in the Yoruba city of Lagos. It uses talking drums and guitars along with complex harmonies. King Sunny Ade's songs include "Choices" and "Wait for Me," both encouraging family planning. He donates royalties from the sale of these songs to the Planned Parenthood Federation. He performs regularly in the United States, singing mostly in Yoruba. Somehow, the rhythm and beat carries his American audiences along even when they don't understand a word.

Fela Kuti

Femi Kuti

In the 1960s, Fela Kuti virtually invented the style known as Afrobeat, which combines African melodies and rhythms and then mixes in jazz. Known to everyone as "Fela," he often dealt with serious political issues in his music, including corruption and police brutality. His songs were long events, lasting as much as an hour. Once he had recorded a song, he stopped performing it so his concerts were always fresh and exciting. Fela died of AIDS in 1997.

Fela's son, Femi Kuti, grew up with the music, hearing it his whole life. He joined his father's band when he was still a teenager and now has created his own legend in the world of music. He tours in Europe and the United States, including a sold-out performance at Irving Plaza in New York City. Femi's music may prove to be even more popular than his father's because he chooses subjects that have a wider appeal. He received the Best-Selling African Artist award at the 2000 World Music Awards.

Jos National Museum

When tin miners working in the Jos area began finding pottery and terra-cotta figures from the Nok culture, they discovered the ancient roots of some of the earliest people who lived in Nigeria. These pieces are now at the Jos National Museum, founded by William Fagg and continued by his daughter, Angela Fagg Rackham. The museum is part of a complex that includes four separate museums as well as a zoo.

Super Sports

In Africa, soccer, which is known as football, is the number one sport. In Nigeria, it is the activity that could unite this fractured nation. The country put together a great national team that competed in the 1996 Summer Olympics and won a gold medal, thanks to its star player, Nwankwo Kanu.

The Nigerian soccer team lines up.

Soccer is not confined to men. Nigeria also has a national women's soccer team, created in 1991, that has competed in the Women's World Cup, an international sporting event that some consider more important than the Olympics. Even some Muslim girls have been trying to play; although they encounter tremendous opposition. In addition to soccer, Nigerian women ran off with medals in world events including the 100-meter hurdles and the 400-meter relay.

A surprising category for Nigeria is weight lifting, in which Nigerian women recently competed for the first time. Ruth Ogbeifo won a silver medal for Nigeria in the 2000 Summer Olympics in the women's heavyweight category.

Nigeria qualifies in the women's weight lifting finals at the Sydney Olympic Games.

Glory Alozie competes in the 100-meter hurdles in the 2000 Summer Olympics.

Nigeria won two other silver medals in track. Glory Alozie took home the silver for the women's 100-meter hurdles. In the men's 400-meter team relay, the four-member team also won a bronze medal. The four runners were Sunday Bada, Clement Chukwu, Jude Monye, and Enefiok Udo-Obong.

Durbar Festival

Twice a year, Muslims in the north stage a great festival known as a *durbar*. This festival marks two major occasions in a Muslim's life. One is held at the end of Ramadan, the Muslim holy month of fasting and prayer. The other takes place at the time of the pilgrimage to Mecca, called the *haij*. Most durbars are held by the Hausa and the Fulani, people of the north, and they take place throughout the region.

The occasion combines a display of horsemanship with material splendor. Men on horses with elaborate saddles, beautiful bridles, and reins covered with embroidery and golden decorations ride through the streets of the towns. Men wearing turbans, sometimes with their faces veiled, pay honor to the emirs. The costumes glitter in the hot sun, and the enormous amount of fabric used for each rider's garments gives a sense of the wealth of people. The costumes look like they're from another century, and that is quite accurate. They reflect a very old tradition, and this helps to tie the people of the twenty-first century with their ancestors and with their traditional rulers.

Argungu Fishing Festival

Once a year, the Sokoto River in northwest Nigeria becomes a festival site for fishing. Along a mile-long stretch of the river, which is off-limits for the rest of the year, fishermen from the whole region come to compete and show off their skills. At a signal, the fishermen jump into the muddy waters carrying big butterfly nets and calabashes—calabash is dried gourds

Men on horses in a durbar festival

Argungu Fishing Festival

used to scoop up the fish. They also use their hands and their nets to catch fish in the crowded river. Mainly, they catch huge Nile perch.

Fishing isn't the only activity. The festival, which takes place at harvest time, includes music, drumming, and dancing. The Argungu Fishing Festival dates back to the early 1900s and is believed to celebrate the end of an argument between two rulers in the area.

Contemporary sculptors and artists tell the story of Nigeria too, through their works in wood and paint. Fonshu, a sculptor, creates an entire story that can be read from bottom to top in his sculpture. Each level of the wooden sculpture tells part of the story. His work is very complicated, but if you know Nigerian legends, it is easy to read. And even if you can't "read" the story, you can admire the skill with which he carved it and enjoy looking at the figures of Nigerian people.

Fonshu at work

Country Life, City Life

116

Yoruba women wait for a ride to the market to sell their yams.

THERE HAS BEEN A STEADY FLOW OF PEOPLE FROM THE rural areas into the major cities of Nigeria. As recently as ten years ago, 70 percent of the people still lived in small farming villages. By the year 2000, about half of the people lived in cities. As much as 15 to 20 percent of the entire population live in just two cities, Lagos and Ibadan.

Today, Nigeria has the highest proportion of people in Africa living in cities. But even in the cities, they maintain their cultural identities and follow their traditions very closely. Family ties and relationships are the strongest bonds. These ties are reinforced by ceremonies, especially weddings.

Opposite: **Skyline of Lagos as seen from the expressway**

Country Life, City Life **117**

Nike in her neighborhood

School in Lagos

Children are more likely to go to school in the big cities. Olanike Olakunri is a typical Yoruba city girl. Her friends and family call her by her nickname, Nike (pronounced *Nee-kee*). Each day her mother takes her to school before going off to her own business.

Nike's school day includes classes in arithmetic, English, and reading. In the rural areas, most children start school speaking their own language, such as Hausa, which they learn at home from their families. Around the third grade, all children start to study in English, which is the official language of Nigeria.

School is supposed to be free and compulsory for all Nigerian children, and the Constitution of 1999 says that all children should have free schooling all the way through university. Some parents who want to be sure their children get a good education pay for extra studies. Although schooling is free, parents must still pay for school uniforms and other

National Holidays in Nigeria

New Year's Day	January 1
Good Friday	March or April
Easter Monday	March or April
May Day	May 1
Independence Day	October 1
Christmas	December 25 and 26

Schoolchildren in Osmalla

extras. When a family has many children, it often becomes too difficult to send them all, or to send them for more than a few years.

Students like Nike also enjoy the many activities that go on in a big city, such as a food festival that was held in Lagos. Foods from around Nigeria were shown, and a dietitian explained how they were prepared. Many schools sent classes to the festival to learn about the other parts of their country. This was a great way to help the students in Lagos feel more connected to the other people and regions of their country.

A food festival where students learn about good nutrition

They also show off their talents in competitions. There are music contests in which children perform the local songs and dances, and even a poetry contest, which was won one year by fourteen-year-old Uloma Agbugba. Her poem expressed her hopes for her country and was judged the best from all the poems written by children throughout the country. Competitors from every state were judged in this national competition.

Children's poetry contest winner

The Ayo Game

All over Africa, children and adults play a board game that has different names in different countries. In Nigeria, it's called the *ayo game*. The board, which looks like an open egg container, has several sections, usually twelve or fourteen, although there can be as many as sixty.

Two people play the game, using seeds, stones, marbles, or any round objects. The person who ends up with the most seeds—or other objects—wins the game. Four seeds are placed in each of the twelve cups. The first player scoops up all the seeds in one cup and then moves around the board, placing one seed in each cup until they are used up. If the last seed lands in an opponent's cup, the player captures all the seeds in that cup and puts them in his "bank." The game continues until one player has no more seeds.

A woman has her hair braided at an outdoor salon.

Hair Braiding

Braiding hair into intricate and beautiful patterns is a very old tradition in Nigeria. These hairstyles can be seen on the ancient Benin sculptures, where every aspect of the hair is worked out in great detail. Women and girls spend hours patiently sitting while their hair is braided by experts. Hairdressers often have pictures showing the styles they can do.

Many Babies

Women in Nigeria have large families, with an average of six children. This is one of the highest birthrates in the world. Many children do not live to see their first birthday because of disease, poor nutrition, dirty drinking water, and not enough medical facilities.

It is not unusual for someone to grow up in a Muslim household where the father has four wives and twenty children are competing for food and attention. Girls in the rural areas rarely receive more than a primary education and are married very young. They begin having children when they are teenagers. From time to time the government has tried to encourage a lower birthrate by offering birth control information and contraceptives. These are difficult to supply in areas where the men control access to clinics or don't allow them to operate at all.

Going to a Wedding

In Lagos, a wedding is more than a celebration of a marriage. It is a uniquely Nigerian way to celebrate a culture. Weddings are also an important social occasion. They help people who live busy city lives stay in touch and keep their relationships very close.

At a modern Yoruba wedding between wealthy families, the women prepare well in advance by making dresses for the occasion. Both sides of the family get together to decide on the colors of the clothing that they are going to wear. When the wedding invitation arrives, it even includes the colors they have chosen. All the guests then wear clothes of those colors. One woman will choose a fabric and then send lengths of it to the other women in her family so they can make matching dresses for the occasion.

When guests greet the bride and groom, they make a big show of giving money. They usually take the bills and fan them out in front of the bride. They might even stick some bills on the bride's forehead while everyone is dancing. Then a friend of the bride gathers up the money in a basket. Nigerian weddings are very expensive, and this is a way to pay back the family for all the money they've spent.

Giving money at a wedding

Life in the North

Hausa people coming home from market

In the northern third of Nigeria, where there is little rainfall, life is very difficult. Water is the biggest daily concern of the people there. Women and children walk great distances to wells where they fill up buckets and carry them home.

The Hausa-Fulani, who dominate the north, grow their own food, using the small amount of rain that falls. They have learned how to grow millet, a kind of grain, as well as corn, cotton, and peanuts. They often sell the peanuts at a local market.

According to Islamic laws, women and men are separated in much of their daily lives. If boys and girls are not allowed to attend the same school, it is likely that only boys will receive an education.

This area has few health facilities. Because women are not allowed to see male doctors, their health problems are often left untreated.

Cattle

In Africa, cattle are a sign of wealth. Keeping a large herd of cattle is a way of showing this wealth, the way other people keep money in the bank. In Nigeria, more than 90 percent of the cattle are raised in the north because it is the only region of the country that is free of the dreaded tsetse fly. This little insect carries diseases that are fatal to cattle.

These cattle are zebu, which are best suited to the dry, hot climate. Many of them are owned by the Fulani. The Fulani

A cattle herdsman in northern Nigeria

are nomads who move their homes and herds from place to place, looking for water and grazing. The north is the major supplier of cattle to Nigeria's meat industry. Hausa Muslims are the butchers throughout Nigeria because cattle must be slaughtered in a ritual way that allows Muslims to eat the meat. This is referred to as *halal*.

Learning through Proverbs

Amusing sayings, known as proverbs, are part of most of the cultures in Nigeria. Proverbs are ways of teaching lessons or reminding people that their actions may have consequences they didn't intend. Some proverbs are very easy to understand while others are difficult to figure out. Here are some examples:

Igbo Proverb:

"When you are eating with the devil, you must use a long spoon." (In other words, be careful about the company you keep.)

Yoruba Proverb:

"When the door is closed, you must learn to slide across the crack of the sill." (In other words, no matter how many obstacles are placed in your way, you must find ways to overcome them.)

This Yoruba proverb illustrates the remarkable way in which Nigerians live, work, and survive. In spite of the many difficulties and changes this nation has faced over the years, its people always make the best of what they have. It's what Nigeria must continue to do in order to find a way to improve the lives of all its people.

Timeline

Nigerian History		World History	
		2500 B.C.	Egyptians build the Pyramids and Sphinx in Giza.
Nok people are living in Nigeria.	About 500 B.C.– A.D. 200	563 B.C.	Buddha is born in India.
		A.D. 313	The Roman emperor Constantine recognizes Christianity.
		610	The prophet Muhammad begins preaching a new religion called Islam.
Yoruba people are living west of the Niger River.	About 1000	1054	The Eastern (Orthodox) and Western (Roman) Churches break apart.
		1066	William the Conqueror defeats the English in the Battle of Hastings.
		1095	Pope Urban II proclaims the First Crusade.
Fulani people are in northern Nigeria.	About 1200	1215	King John seals the Magna Carta.
		1300s	The Renaissance begins in Italy.
		1347	The Black Death sweeps through Europe.
Benin people are living in southern Nigeria; Hausa kingdom is flourishing in the north.	About 1400	1453	Ottoman Turks capture Constantinople, conquering the Byzantine Empire.
Portuguese traders and explorers reach the coast of Nigeria.	1471	1492	Columbus arrives in North America.
Borno Kingdom absorbs part of Hausaland.	Late 1500s	1500s	The Reformation leads to the birth of Protestantism.
Drought causes a famine that wipes out the Borno.	Mid-1700s	1776	The Declaration of Independence is signed.
		1789	The French Revolution begins.
Lagos becomes a British colony; British take over most of Yorubaland.	1861	1865	The American Civil War ends.
British give George Goldie rights to trade in the Niger basin.	1879		
Britain begins a plan of indirect rule.	1900		
Britain unites the southern and northern protectorates of Nigeria.	1914	1914	World War I breaks out.
Nigerians aid Britain in World War I.	1914–1918	1917	The Bolshevik Revolution brings Communism to Russia.
Herbert Macauley forms the Nigerian National Democratic Party.	1923	1929	Worldwide economic depression begins.

Nigerian History

Royal Dutch/Shell begins exploring for oil in Nigeria.	1937
Nigerian Youth Movement calls for Nigerian self-government.	1938
About 100,000 Nigerians fight on Britain's side during World War II.	1939–1945
Nigerians work to gain independence for their country.	1946–1959
Nigeria's first commercial oil field is found.	1956
Nigeria gains independence.	1960
Nigeria becomes a republic.	1963
Nigerian politics has a pattern of elections followed by military coups.	1966–1999
Nigeria has a civil war over Biafra's independence.	1967–1970
Nigeria joins the organization of Petroleum Exporting Countries (OPEC).	1971
Nigeria hosts the Festival of Pan-African Culture.	1977
Nigeria becomes dependent on income from petroleum production and goes into debt when worldwide oil prices drop.	1985
Wole Soyinka becomes the first African to win the Nobel Prize for Literature.	1986
Sani Abacha rules Nigeria by fraud, theft, and murder.	1993–1998
Nine men are executed for championing the rights of the Ogoni people in the oil-rich Delta Region.	1995
Nigeria's soccer team wins a gold medal at the Olympic Games.	1996
Olusegun Obasanjo becomes Nigeria's first elected president since 1979.	1999
Nigeria's government sends more money back to the Ogoni people in the Delta Region; the United States sends troops to train Nigerian peacekeepers.	2000

World History

1939	World War II begins, following the German invasion of Poland.
1945	World War II ends.
1957	The Vietnam War starts.
1969	Humans land on the moon.
1975	The Vietnam War ends.
1979	Soviet Union invades Afghanistan.
1983	Drought and famine in Africa.
1989	The Berlin Wall is torn down, as Communism crumbles in Eastern Europe.
1991	Soviet Union breaks into separate states.
1992	Bill Clinton is elected U.S. president.
2000	George W. Bush is elected U.S. president.

Fast Facts

Official name: Federal Republic of Nigeria

Capital: Abuja

Official language: English

Lagos

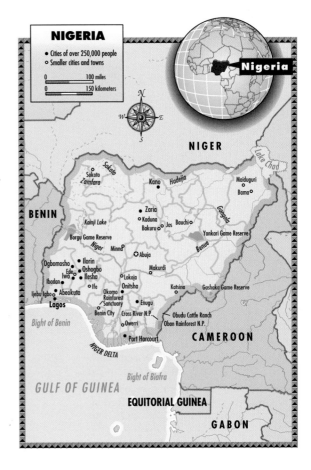

Nigeria's flag

Jos Plateau

Official religion: None

Year of founding: 1963

National anthem: *Arise, O Compatriots, Nigeria's Call Obey*

Government: Federal republic

Chief of state: President

Head of government: President

Area: 356,695 square miles (923,768 sq km)

Dimensions: East–west, 360 miles (579 km)
North–south, 976 miles (1,571 km)

Latitude and longitude of geographic center: 10° North, 8° East

Land and water borders: Gulf of Guinea to the south, Benin to the west, Niger to the north, Lake Chad to the northeast, Chad and Cameroon to the east

Highest elevation: 6,699 feet (2,042 m) in the Cameroon Highlands

Lowest elevation: Sea level along the Gulf of Guinea

Average temperature extremes: 68°F (20°C) in Port Harcourt;
100°F (38°C) in Maiduguri

Average precipitation extremes: 20 inches (50 cm) in the north;
160 inches (400 cm) in the southeast

National population (2000 est.): 123,337,822

Livestock on the savanna

Currency

Population of largest cities (2001 est):

Lagos	8–13,000,000
Ibadan	5,000,000
Kano	1,000,000
Ogbomosho	800,000
Oshogbo	500,000

Famous landmarks:

▶ *Balogun Market*, in Lagos

▶ *Cross River National Park*, southeastern Nigeria

▶ *Gashaka Gumpti National Park*, in the east

▶ *Jos Museum*, in Jos

▶ *Kainji Lake National Park*, western Nigeria

▶ *National Museum*, in Lagos

▶ *Okumu Nature Sanctuary*, near Benin City

▶ *Old Quarters of Hausa cities*, in Kano and Zaria

▶ *Old Quarters of Yoruba cities*, in Oyo and Ife

▶ *Yankari National Park*, east-central Nigeria

▶ *Zuma Rock*, near Abuja

Industry: Nigeria is one of the world's leading oil exporters. In 1971, Nigeria's government formed a national oil corporation and joined the Organization of Petroleum Exporting Countries (OPEC). Other important mining products include limestone, marble, tin, and coal. Manufacturing makes up the second-largest part of Nigeria's economy. The government has begun steel, chemical, and pulp and paper industries. Textiles, food products, and cement are other important products.

Currency: Nigeria's monetary unit is the *naira*, which equals 100 *kobo*. Exchange rate in April 2001: U.S.$1 U.S. = 129 naira.

Schoolchildren

Chinua Achebe

System of weights and measures: Metric system

Literacy (1995 est.): 57 percent

Common Hausa words and phrases:

Ina ine. (ee-nay ee-nee)	Good evening.
Ina kwana. (ee-nay kwah-nah)	Good morning.
Ina labari? (ee-nay lah-bah-ree)	What's the news?
Kazo lafiya? (kah-zoh lah-fee-yah)	What's your name?
Lafiya lau. (lay-fee-yay lay-u)	I'm fine.
Sanu. (sah-nuh)	Hello.
Nawa nawa ne? (nah-wah nah-wah nee)	How much?

Famous Nigerians:

Moshood K. O. Abiola *Political leader*	(1937–1998)
Chinua Achebe *Writer*	(1930–)
King Sunny Ade *Musician*	(1946–)
Tafawa Balewa *Political leader*	(1912–1966)
Usman dan Fodio *Muslim religious leader*	(1754–1817)
Olusegun Obasanjo *President*	(1937–)
Ken Saro-Wiwa *Writer, political activist*	(1941–1995)
Wole Soyinka *Playwright*	(1934–)

To Find Out More

Nonfiction

▶ Adeeb, Hassan, and Bonnetta Adeeb. *Nigeria: One Nation, Many Cultures*. Exploring Cultures of the World. New York: Benchmark Books, 1998.

▶ Barker, Carol. *A Family in Nigeria*. Minneapolis: Lerner Publications, 1985.

▶ Blauer, Ettagale. *Nigeria, Children of the World*. Milwaukee: Gareth Stevens, 1992.

▶ *The World Factbook 2000*. Washington, D.C.: CIA, 2000.

▶ *Encyclopedia Britannica*. Micropedia, Macropedia, Yearbook, and Online. 2000.

▶ Else, David, et al. *West Africa*. Hawthorn, Australia: Lonely Planet Publications, 1999.

▶ Levy, Patricia. *Nigeria. Cultures of the World*. New York: Benchmark Books, 1993.

▶ Metz, Helen Chapin, ed. *Nigeria: A Country Study*. Washington, D.C.: Library of Congress, 1992.

▶ Trillo, Richard and Jim Hudgens. *West Africa: The Rough Guide*. London: The Rough Guides, 1999.

▶ U.S. State Department. *Background Notes: Nigeria*. Washington, D.C., August 2000.

Fiction

▶ Achebe, Chinua. *Things Fall Apart*. New York: Anchor Books, 1994.

▶ Buchi, Emecheta. *Slave Girl*. New York: George Braziller, 1980.

▶ Okri, Ben. *The Famished Road*. New York: Bantam, 1993.

▶ Walker, Barbara K., and Helen Siegl. *The Dancing Palm Tree and Other Nigerian Folktales*. Lubbock, Texas: Texas Tech University, 1991.

Websites

▶ **Motherland Nigeria**
http://www.motherlandnigeria.com/kidzone.html
This site provides information about Nigeria's food, people, geography, and government plus stories and games.

▶ **Interactive World Fact Book**
http://www.georgraphic.org/maps/nigeria_maps.htm
Current information about Nigeria plus maps.

▶ **About Nigeria**
http://www.emulateme.com/nigeria.htm
Information about Nigeria's government, economy, and people plus lyrics to the national anthem.

Organizations and Embassies

▶ **Nigeria High Commission**
295 Metcalfe Street
Ottawa, Canada K2P1R9
(613) 236-0521

▶ **Embassy of Nigeria**
2210 M Street, N.W.
Washington, D.C. 20037
(202) 822-1539
http://www.nigeria-government.com

Index

Page numbers in *italics* indicate illustrations.

Meet the Authors

Eᴛᴛᴀɢᴀʟᴇ Bʟᴀᴜᴇʀ ᴀɴᴅ Jᴀꜱᴏɴ Lᴀᴜʀé first visited Nigeria in 1974. "We began in Morocco and headed south. Before we knew it, we were caught in a sandstorm in the Sahara. Driving across Africa is the most amazing way to see the continent and to appreciate the vastness of it. Each time we entered another country, we saw completely different ways of life and that was certainly true in Nigeria. We entered Nigeria from the neighboring country of Niger. They're both named after the Niger River, which can be pretty confusing. But in Niger, the people speak

French because it was once a French colony. As soon as you cross the border into Nigeria, the people speak English because it used to be a British colony. It's like having a history lesson come to life.

"For a country with so many people in it, the countryside is pretty sparsely populated, but even at the border, where we had to go through customs, there were men dressed in beautiful flowing robes. As soon as we started to drive south into Nigeria, we could see houses dotting the countryside—round houses with thatched roofs. Soon enough, we plunged into the noise and traffic of Kano. Even in Kano, we saw women carrying everything on their heads. It was amazing to see the height of things piled up there. Even little children carry huge things. It was a fascinating experience."

Photo Credits